# DESIGNING DATABASES

## Nev Glynn

BSc DipEd GradDipEd (CompEd) MEd

## Shiron Dixon

BSc DipEd GradDipEd (CompEd) BEdStud MEd

NELSON
CENGAGE Learning™

Australia • Brazil • Japan • Korea • Mexico •
Singapore • Spain • United Kingdom • United States

**Designing Databases**
**1st Edition**
**Nev Glynn**
**Shiron Dixon**

Acquisitions editor: Paul Brock
Production editor: Elaine Myors, Anna Crago
Text design: April Briscoe
Cover design: Diane Booth
Illustrator: Diane Booth
Typeset in Palatino by Midland Typesetters, Victoria

Any URLs contained in this publication were checked for currency during the production process. Note, however, that the publisher cannot vouch for the ongoing currency of URLs.

First published 1997 by McGraw Hill Australia.
This edition published in 2010 by Cengage Learning Australia.

**Acknowledgements**
Additional owners of copyright material are named in on-page credits.

For product information and technology assistance,
in Australia call **1300 790 853**;
in New Zealand call **0800 449 725**

For permission to use material from this text or product, please email
**aust.permissions@cengage.com**

ISBN 978 0 17 021113 0

**Cengage Learning Australia**
Level 7, 80 Dorcas Street
South Melbourne, Victoria Australia 3205

**Cengage Learning New Zealand**
Unit 4B Rosedale Office Park
331 Rosedale Road, Albany, North Shore 0632, NZ

For learning solutions, visit **cengage.com.au**

Printed in China by RR Donnelley Asia Printing Solutions Limited.
1 2 3 4 5 6 7 14 13 12 11 10

# Contents

Preface ............................................................................................ v

Introduction .................................................................................... vi

**CHAPTER 1**

System architecture ........................................................................ 1

A conceptual information system ..................................................... 2

**CHAPTER 2**

Conceptual schema design process ................................................. 10

**STEP 1** Convert examples to elementary facts ..................................... 11
   Arity ............................................................................................ 11
   Elementary facts ........................................................................ 12
   Significant output reports ......................................................... 16
**STEP 2** Draw the fact types ..................................................................... 21
   Ternary facts ............................................................................. 23
   Multiple fact types .................................................................... 24
   Population check ....................................................................... 30
**STEP 3** Check for entity types that should be combined .................... 32
**STEP 4** Add uniqueness constraints and check arity of fact types ........... 37
   Uniqueness constraints on unary fact types ........................... 37
   Uniqueness constraints on binary fact types ......................... 39
   Determining uniqueness constraints ....................................... 44
   Uniqueness constraints on longer fact types ......................... 48
   Arity check ................................................................................. 50
   Assumptions ............................................................................... 52
   External uniqueness constraints .............................................. 58
**STEP 5** Add mandatory constraints ....................................................... 60
   Disjunctive mandatory roles .................................................... 63
   Reference schemes ..................................................................... 69
**STEP 6** Check for arithmetic and logical derivations ......................... 72
   Arithmetic derivations .............................................................. 73
   Logical derivations .................................................................... 74
**STEP 7** Add other constraints ................................................................ 78
   Value constraints ....................................................................... 78
   Frequency constraints ............................................................... 79
   Subset constraints ..................................................................... 79
   Equality constraints .................................................................. 80

Exclusion constraints ....................................................................... 81
Subtype constraints ......................................................................... 82
**STEP 8** Perform final checks ............................................................... 86

**CHAPTER 3**

# Relational implementation ................................... 90

The relational model ................................................................................. 90
The relational mapping procedure ........................................................ 93
**STEP 1** Compound uniqueness constraints ........................................ 93
**STEP 2** Simple uniqueness constraints ............................................... 94
**STEP 3** Constraints ................................................................................. 94
Nested fact types ............................................................................. 95
One-to-one fact types ..................................................................... 96
Subtypes ........................................................................................... 97

Glossary .......................................................................... 106
Answers .......................................................................... 109
Index .............................................................................. 145

# Preface

This book is written to provide a step-by-step approach to designing relational databases.

It is intended for use by students studying database development, specifically students of the information system topic of the Queensland senior secondary subject Information Processing and Technology, the major aspects of the Developing Custom Databases Unit of the new Queensland Board registered subject Computer Studies, and tertiary students. It assumes that students and teachers have knowledge of the software development cycle as applied to database development namely:

- problem definition
- solution specification
- design
- implementation
- testing
- evaluation
- documentation.

This book addresses the design phase of this cycle, in preparation for the design's implementation in an appropriate software. It does not attempt to provide coverage of the other phases.

We want to thank Alison, Erica and Daniel Glynn and Owen Dixon for their patience and support during the development of this book. Sincere thanks must go to Paul Shield and Doug Carey for their advice and encouragement. Thanks, too, to Terry Halpin for his work in this area.

## About the authors

**Nev Glynn** is the Head of Computing at Clayfield College, Brisbane. Nev has been involved in teaching the senior subject Information Processing and Technology since its initial development, and is the State Review Panel Chair of the panel that reviews student work in that subject. Nev has been a statewide consultant for Information Processing and Technology for the Queensland Department of Education.

**Shiron Dixon** is the Head of Department (Mathematics) at Mitchelton State High School, Brisbane. Shiron was, for several years, the Review Officer (Information Processing and Technology) at the Board of Secondary School Studies, assisting teachers with work program development, assessment practices and maintenance of standards in student work.

Both Nev and Shiron have been involved in part-time lecturing to Technology Education students at the Queensland University of Technology (Kelvin Grove).

# Introduction

We live in an information rich age. We are becoming increasingly more reliant on accessing information electronically. The accuracy and completeness of the information we receive is dependant not only on our searching skills (how well we can formulate queries), but also on the way in which the data has been analysed and stored. This means that the design of information systems is critically important in terms of its accuracy and ease of use.

The design of an information system is a complex process. Considerations when designing information systems include hardware, software, people, processes and data. This text looks at the data for an information system and how it can be organised using data modelling to ensure the efficient storage of this data. The data storage aspect of an information system is usually referred to as the **database**. Hence the title of this text—*Designing Databases*.

We have deliberately avoided the use of acronyms, which are quite common in this field of study. In general they do not improve communication and are a legacy of poor typing skills of the past. Where an acronym is widely used in other references it is identified but not used continually.

Database design has its own precise language. You'll see words and phrases recurring throughout this book. Don't be daunted by the terminology. A glossary has been included, but there are some terms that are essential for understanding. The **universe of discourse** is one of these terms. The universe of discourse (UoD) is the domain of information being discussed by the client and the database designer, who is often referred to as the **universe of discourse expert**. It is essential the designer and client have the same view of the universe of discourse for the design to fulfil the needs of the client.

The approach to database design taken here is the use of Object-Role Modelling (ORM) which treats components of the universe of discourse as objects that play roles. The version of Object-Role Modelling used is based on the extensions to the Natural language Information Analysis Method (NIAM) pioneered by Professor G. M. Nijssen in the early 1970s and since formalised and refined by Dr T. A. Halpin from the University of Queensland. Although the version used is essentially the Natural language Information Analysis Method it has been modified for use with secondary school students. A tertiary coverage of the entire methodology is found in *Conceptual Schema & Relational Database Design* Second Edition by Terry Halpin.

Presenting the database design process has been approached by firstly considering the architecture for representing the data contained in information systems. This introduces the idea of a conceptual model of a database without the formalisation of diagrammatic representation. The relationship between the conceptual view and the eventual implementation of the database is explained. Next a step-by-step procedure for creating **conceptual schema diagrams** is presented. This is done in considerable detail with many opportunities for the reader to practise the steps. Finally, a method to transform the conceptual schema to a set of relational table definitions that can be directly implemented on today's systems is provided. Answers for all exercises are to be found at the back of the text.

**CHAPTER ❶**

# System architecture

The data in an information system can be viewed on four levels: conceptual, logical, internal and external. The **conceptual schema** specifies the structure of the universe of discourse. It describes the objects contained in the universe of discourse, the roles these objects play and the constraints affecting these objects. The conceptual schema allows communication about the specific universe of discourse. It ensures a common language for the domain expert and the database designer, by requiring the same meaning for the words being used.

Current technologies require that we convert the conceptual schema to some lower level structure to enable it to be implemented. In a particular situation, an appropriate model is selected, such as the relational model used in this text, and the resultant mapping of the conceptual schema results in the **logical schema**. The logical schema expresses the universe of discourse in terms of the data structures and operators specific to the chosen model.

The logical schema can then be implemented in a specific system that implements the model. This description of the universe of discourse that specifies details about the storage of data and access structures used is an **internal schema**. Since a number of different database management systems could be chosen, a logical schema may be expressed as a number of different internal schema. The internal schema is the only aspect that needs change when implementing an information system on different computer systems.

Additionally, an **external schema** specifies how a particular user views the universe of discourse and how it relates to the conceptual schema. Some users will be restricted to only sections of the database. This may be to simplify a user's job, since it is easier to formulate queries on a database when only necessary information (without any extraneous information) is available. Alternatively, for security reasons, it may be preferable to allow only certain users access to sensitive information.

# A conceptual information system

To become more familiar with the workings of a conceptual schema we will first consider a conceptual information system. A conceptual information system is a view of a database at the conceptual level only. This eliminates implementation detail and allows concentration on the components of the system. The conceptual information system consists of the conceptual schema, the conceptual database and the **conceptual information processor**.

The conceptual schema specifies the permitted states and changes of the system. For the conceptual information processor, the conceptual schema will be specified using four headings:
- reference scheme
- stored fact types
- constraints
- derivation rules.

The **reference scheme** lists the objects of the universe of discourse and how they are identified (e.g. Person (First Name), Subject (Subject Name)). The **stored fact types** section lists all the acceptable types of sentences (e.g. Person studies Subject). The **constraints** section lists all rules that place restrictions on the stored data and on the changing of data. The **derivation rules** specify information that is not stored directly but can be generated from the existing data. An example of a conceptual schema for a particular school follows. Note that this school may operate quite differently from those you may be used to.

## Reference scheme
Student (First Name), Teacher (Surname), Subject (Subject Name), Room (Number)

## Stored fact types

Student studies Subject
Teacher is teacher of Subject
Teacher teaches in Room

## Constraints

C1—each Student studies at most 6 Subjects
C2—a Student studies a Subject only once
C3—each Teacher teaches some Subject
C4—each Teacher is teacher of, at most, one Subject
C5—each Teacher teaches in some Room
C6—each Teacher teaches in, at most, one Room
C7—each Subject has only one Teacher

## Derivation rules

D1—Teacher T teaches Student S if T is teacher of X and S studies X
D2—Student S attends Room R if X teaches S and X teaches in R
D3—NrSubjects (Student S) = Select count (Subject) from Studies where
Student = S

The derivation rules use variables to represent values found in the database. All instances (or occurrences) of the same variable must have the same value in the one rule. The fact type being used is identified by the verb used in the sentence. In the D3 statement, S is a variable. The statement indicates that the number of Subjects studied by a student (e.g. S) can be determined by counting the number of Subjects that have S listed as studying the Subject. Values in the database are characters, a sequence of characters or numbers. In this text a traditional computer science approach will be used in denoting the difference between characters and numbers. Characters and strings of characters will be enclosed in single quotation marks and numbers will be written without quotes.

The conceptual database contains the instances that populate the information system, for example:

'Kathy' studies 'English'
'Paul' studies 'English'
'Mary' studies 'Mathematics'
'Cassy' studies 'Geography'
'Paul' studies 'Geography'
'Smith' is teacher of 'Geography'
'Smith' teaches in 'G104'
'Grypes' is teacher of 'English'
'Grypes' teaches in 'E203'
'Brown' is teacher of 'Mathematics'
'Brown' teaches in 'A103'

The conceptual information processor is that part of the system responsible for enforcing the conceptual schema when changes are made to the data. The user interacts with the conceptual information processor by making a **transaction**. A transaction may be either an instruction or a question. The conceptual information processor responds by accepting or rejecting an instruction or by answering or rejecting queries. Instructions, which will be limited to add or delete, will be rejected if they violate the constraints and queries will be rejected if they are illegal.

For example, if the user enters:
add 'Cassy' studies 'English'
the conceptual information processor would respond with:
accepted.

The following shows a user's session maintaining the database.

| *User* | *Conceptual information processor* |
|---|---|
| add 'Kathy' studies 'English' | rejected—C2 violated |
| add 'Cassy' studies 'Mathematics' | accepted |
| add 'Brown' teaches in 'B104' | rejected—C6 violated |
| add 'Kathy' studies 'Science' | accepted |
| add 'Mary' achieved 'VHA' | rejected—unknown fact type |
| delete 'Kathy' studies 'Science' | accepted |
| delete 'Smith' teaches in 'G104' | rejected—C5 violated |
| add 'Green' is teacher of 'Science' | rejected—C5 violated |
| add 'Green' teaches in 'S104' | rejected—C3 violated |

The last two entries in the previous table are an attempt to add a new teacher to the database. The attempt failed as each of the transactions failed. Each violated a constraint; *add 'Green' is teacher of 'Science'* was not accepted as Green would then be a teacher without a room and *add 'Green' teaches in 'S104'* was not accepted as Green would then be a teacher without a subject. If both transactions were accepted the new teacher would have a subject and a room and no constraint would be violated. This leads to the need for compound transactions. 'Begin' and 'End' are used to show the start and finish of compound transactions. The conceptual information processor considers the effect of the entire compound transaction, not each individual transaction. For example:
Begin
'Green' is teacher of 'Science'
'Green' teaches in 'S104'
End
This example would be accepted by the conceptual information processor.

So far we have only considered transactions that are instructions. Transactions can also pose questions (queries) as well as accessing functions from the derivation rules. Examples of these types of transactions appear in the following table, along with the conceptual information processor's response.

| User | Conceptual information processor |
|------|----------------------------------|
| 'Cassy' studies 'Geography'? | Yes |
| 'Cassy' studies 'English'? | No |
| which Teacher is teacher of 'English'? | Grypes |
| which Teacher is teacher of 'History'? | No Teacher |
| which Student studies 'English'? | Kathy |
|  | Paul |
| NrSubjects ('Paul') | 2 |
| which Student attends 'E203'? | Kathy |
|  | Paul |
| which Teacher teaches 'Mary'? | Brown |
| which 'Smith' teaches Student? | Cassy |
|  | Paul |

The last transaction may require some explanation. The derivation rule D1 has two places in which a value can be supplied. In the query *which Teacher is teacher of 'English'?*, the known value is supplied for the second value in the fact and the question reads quite well. But in the query *which 'Smith' teaches Student*, the known value is placed in the first position, which makes the query strange but does not make it wrong. The query is actually asking *which Student is taught by 'Smith'?*, but the *is taught by* is not defined in the derivation rules so cannot be used. This could be remedied by adding the following derivation rule.

D4—Student S is taught by Teacher T if T teaches S

**Note:** D4 uses D1 as part of its definition.

## EXERCISE ❶

### Question I

The following conceptual schema is concerned with sporting information in a school.

### Reference scheme

Person (Surname), Sport (Name), Age (Number), Gender (F/M)

### Stored fact types

Person does Sport
Person is Age
Person is Gender
Person captains Sport

## Constraints
C1—each Person is of exactly one Age
C2—a Person does a Sport only once
C3—each Person is some Gender
C4—each Person is at most one Gender
C5—each Sport has only one captain for each gender
C6—Ages range from 13 to 18

## Derivation rules
D1—Person X plays Sport S if X does S or X captains S
D2—Person X plays with Person Y if X plays S and Y plays S and X is G and Y is G
D3—Person X is older than Person Y if X has A and Y has B and >B
D4—NrSports (Person X) = select count (Sport) from plays where Person = X

The database is empty at this time.

Give the conceptual information processor's response to the transactions. It will be useful to update your copy of the conceptual database (i.e. the sentences that are stored). Remember that the response of the conceptual information processor depends on the current state of the database. The following transactions are to be considered as being done consecutively.

(a) add 'Smith' does 'Hockey'
(b) add 'Smith' is of age 15
(c) Begin
        add 'Jones' is of age 15
        add 'Jones' is 'M'
    End
(d) add 'Jones' does 'Hockey'
(e) Begin
        add 'Green' is of age 14
        add 'Green' is 'F'
        add 'Green' captains 'Hockey'
        add 'Green' does 'Touch'
    End
(f) Begin
        add 'Brown' is of age 15
        add 'Brown' is 'F'
        add 'Brown' captains 'Touch'
        add 'Brown' does 'Hockey'
    End
(g) Begin
        add 'Dooley' is of age 14
        add 'Dooley' is 'M'
        add 'Dooley' captains 'Hockey'

```
        add 'Dooley' does 'Cricket'
    End
(h) Begin
        add 'Porter' is of age 13
        add 'Porter' is 'F'
        add 'Alan' is of age 14
        add 'Alan' is 'F'
        add 'Grimes' is of age 15
        add 'Grimes' is 'M'
        add 'Doyle' is of age 16
        add 'Doyle' is 'F'
        add 'Rich' is of age 14
        add 'Rich' is 'M'
        add 'Robertson' is of age 15
        add 'Robertson' is 'F'
        add 'Gibson' is of age 14
        add 'Gibson' is 'F'
    End
(i) Begin
        add 'Porter' does 'Hockey'
        add 'Alan' does 'Hockey'
        add 'Doyle' does 'Hockey'
        add 'Gibson' does 'Hockey'
    End
(j) Begin
        add 'Grimes' does 'Cricket'
        add 'Rich' does 'Cricket'
        add 'Grimes' does 'Hockey'
        add 'Rich' does 'Hockey'
    End
(k) Begin
        add 'Porter' is of age 15
        add 'Porter' is 'M'
    End
(l)  'Green' does 'Touch'?
(m)  'Green' plays 'Hockey'?
(n)  'Green' plays with 'Doyle'?
(o)  'Alan' plays with 'Rich'?
(p)  NrSports ('Dooley')
(q)  which Person plays 'Cricket'?
(r)  'Green' is older than 'Porter'?
(s)  which 'Alan' does Sport?
(t)  which Person is older than 'Robertson'?
(u)  which 'Robertson' plays Sport?
```

(v) which Person captains 'Cricket'?
(w) 'Dooley' plays with 'Rich'?
(x) which Person is of age 14?
(y) delete 'Robertson' is of age 15
(z) which Person plays 'Hockey' and which Person plays 'Touch'?

## Question 2
Assume the following conceptual schema regarding family relationships.

### Reference scheme
Person (Name), Gender (F/M)

### Stored fact types
Person is Gender
Person parent of Person

### Constraints
C1—each Person is some Gender
C2—each Person is at most one Gender
C3—each Person has at most two parents

### Derivation rules
D1—Person X is father of Person Y if X parent of Y and X is 'M'
D2—Person X is mother of Person Y if X parent of Y and X is 'F'
D3—Person X is child of Person Y if Y parent of X

The database is empty at this time.
    Give the conceptual information processor's response to the transactions.
    (a) add 'Jerry' is 'M'
    (b) add 'Mary' is 'F'
    (c) add 'Chris' is 'M'
    (d) add 'Chris' is 'F'
    (e) Begin
        add 'Helen' is 'F'
        add 'Paul' is 'M'
        add 'Barry' is 'M'
        add 'Robyn' is 'F'
        add 'Bradley' is 'M'
        add 'Jerry' parent of 'Helen'
        add 'Mary' parent of 'Helen'
        add 'Chris' parent of 'Jerry'
        add 'Robyn' parent of 'Jerry'
        add 'Barry' parent of 'Chris'
    End
    (f) which Person parent of 'Helen'?
    (g) which Person father of 'Jerry'?

(h) add 'Bradley' parent of 'Helen'
(i) which Person child of 'Barry'?
Devise derivation rules for the following relationships:
(j) is daughter of
(k) is son of
(l) is grandparent of
(m) is grandmother of
(n) is grandfather of
Answer the following question:
(o) The designer is considering adding the following constraint:
C4—each Person has at least one parent
Why would it not be a good idea to add this constraint to the conceptual schema?

**CHAPTER 2**

# Conceptual schema design process

When developing information systems, it is necessary to specify what is required. Object-Role Modelling is a process that describes a universe of discourse in terms of a conceptual schema. This process expresses information in terms of simple facts and is also known as fact-oriented modelling. The facts and constraints are represented graphically. The procedure for designing an Object-Role Modelling conceptual schema is called the conceptual schema design process. The steps of the conceptual schema design process are as follows:

- Step 1—Convert examples to elementary facts
- Step 2—Draw the fact types
- Step 3—Check for entity types that should be combined
- Step 4—Add uniqueness constraints and check arity of fact types
- Step 5—Add mandatory constraints
- Step 6—Check for arithmetic and logical derivations

- Step 7—Add other constraints
- Step 8—Perform final checks

Detailed descriptions of these steps are covered in the following chapters.

 **STEP** ❶

# Convert examples to elementary facts

This step involves expressing information relevant to the universe of discourse as elementary facts. Examples of the sorts of information relevant to the database should be collected. This information might be obtained from a universe of discourse expert—a person familiar with the area of knowledge on which the database is to act. Information may also be determined from output reports and input forms from computerised or manual systems where such reports and forms exist. If a completely new system is being created the designer must extract this information directly from a universe of discourse expert. The input forms and output reports expected would be one way of describing what is to be stored in the system in a form that is easily understood by both the designer and the universe of discourse expert. The universe of discourse expert is an important part of the design of information systems. The conceptual schema design procedure being discussed here allows the universe of discourse to be expressed in English sentences so that the designer and universe of discourse expert can agree before the expensive task of implementation is started.

# Arity

Once the examples have been obtained, they must be expressed as **elementary facts**. An elementary fact states that *an object has a property or that one or more objects are related in a particular way*. The simplest type of elementary fact states that an object plays a role. For example:

**Mary jogs**

This elementary fact states that an object (Mary) plays a particular role (jogs). As there is only one role involved in this fact it is termed a **unary relationship**. The property of a particular fact that describes the number of roles is termed the **arity** of the fact. In this case, the fact has an arity of one. In the vast majority of cases the relationship contains more than one role. For example:

**Mary studies English**

Here Mary plays the role of studying and English plays the role of being studied. The arity of this fact is two and is often called a binary relationship. The arity of a fact can be thought of as the number of holes in which values (representing objects) can be placed, as indicated in the following representation.

| Fact | Arity |
|------|-------|
| Mary jogs<br>1 | 1 (Unary) |
| Mary studies English<br>1        2 | 2 (Binary) |
| Mary received a B for English<br>1      2      3 | 3 (Ternary) |
| Mary has English in Lesson 1 on Monday<br>1     2      3      4 | 4 (Quaternary) |

## EXERCISE 2

### Question I

Give the arity of the following facts:
- (a) Greg Norman plays golf
- (b) Billy stinks
- (c) Mother bakes cakes on Tuesday
- (d) June lives in Australia
- (e) Mary is left-handed

# Elementary facts

The adjective *elementary* puts a further restriction on the facts. Elementary implies that the facts cannot be broken down into smaller parts and still convey the same information. For example:

    Billy Smith born in 1980 is 190 centimetres tall

is not elementary, as the same information can be expressed in the following two facts:

    Billy Smith was born in 1980
    Billy Smith is 190 centimetres tall

    Elementary facts, in general, do not use conjunctives such as *and, or, not, if* or qualifiers such as *all, some.* The following sentences would not be considered as elementary facts.

    Billy and Mary jog
    Mary swims or jogs
    Sylvia does not jog
    If it is fine, Mary jogs

All people jog somewhere

Some people jog in the city

Elementary facts state that objects play roles. The objects in our examples so far have been expressed as values. Values are often used to represent a particular **entity** (e.g. a person) that is part of the universe of discourse. An entity can be a tangible object such as a person or an abstract object such as the subject English. People often misinterpret the meaning of words. For example the sentence:

April is before May

could be interpreted to mean that the month referred to as April precedes the month referred to as May. But just as easily, this sentence could refer to the girl named April being ahead of the girl named May in a queue. Because of such possibilities of misinterpretation, it is necessary to identify very clearly the entities in our elementary facts.

A three component system is used to identify entities—entity type, reference scheme and value. The **entity type** is the set of all instances. The reference scheme states how the value relates to the entity. The **value** gives a specific example of the entity. For example:

Mary studies English

would become

Student with first name 'Mary' studies Subject with name 'English'

Each section would be classified as follows:

## Entity type
Student    Subject

## Reference scheme
first name    name

## Value
Mary    English

This method of referring to objects significantly increases the complexity in expressing elementary sentences. To simplify the writing of elementary facts, the reference scheme can be shown in brackets after the entity type. For example:

Student (First Name) 'Mary' studies Subject (Name) 'English'

Even this representation can become tedious when the same entity is referred to a number of times, as is the case in universe of discourses of reasonable size. An alternative, less tedious but equally acceptable representation specifies the reference schemes before the facts are stated. For example:

## Reference schemes
Student (first name), Subject (name)

## Facts

Student 'Mary' studies Subject 'English'

Elementary facts show the relationships between entities. The use of values in elementary sentences is to show how the facts relate to the data supplied, often in the form of output reports. Sentences that contain the same entities, reference schemes and roles and differ only in the values do not show different elementary facts. That is, in the above example the fact Student 'Mary' studies Subject 'Geography' would not introduce a new elementary fact. Where possible, the first line of data supplied is used as values in the elementary facts.

When examining an output report, it is important to identify all elementary facts, stating each fact only once. Consider the following output report.

| Name | Car |
|---|---|
| Jones H. | Pajero |
| Smith G. | Lancer |
| Brown R. | Patrol |

An elementary fact from this report is:

Person (Name) 'Jones H.' drives Car (Model) 'Pajero'

The values 'Jones H.' and 'Pajero' show the relationship between the elementary fact and the report. Other values could be used such as 'Smith G.' and 'Lancer', but this would still represent an equally valid interpretation of the above report as the following:

Car (Model) 'Pajero' is driven by Person (Name) 'Jones H.'

Both of the elementary facts above describe the same relationship between a person and a car. These must not be treated as different facts. To allow for this, the reverse role can be included in the following elementary fact.

Person (Name) 'Jones H.' **drives/is driven by** Car (Model) 'Pajero'

This notation gives a complete description of the elementary fact. The information contained in this statement cannot yet be fully utilised by current technologies. Therefore, when writing elementary facts, only one role will be required and the reverse role will be implied. Note here that either of the roles (drives or is driven by) is acceptable.

## EXERCISE ❸

## Question I

Identify which sentences are elementary facts.

(a) Leroy plays for the Bullets.

(b) Mary does not smoke.

(c) Ken and Jerry play Hockey.

(d) Jenny likes chocolate and ice-cream.

(e) Jim flew to Sydney.

(f) Alana flew to Melbourne and then to Sydney.

(g) Mary ate Coco-Pops for breakfast.

(h) Everybody loves somebody sometime.

(i) Rover begs.

(j) I can never see what is in those 3D pictures.

(k) Barry eats all berries.

(l) Does Julie run?

(m) The bear is in the house.

(n) Jan is 160 centimetres tall and 55 kilograms in mass.

## Question 2

Write elementary facts for each of the following output reports.

(a)

| Name | Birth year |
|---|---|
| Alan G. | 1975 |
| Best J. | 1984 |
| Pratt R. | 1964 |

(b)

| Teacher | Form |
|---|---|
| Gremmin T. | 8A |
| Siddell T. | 11C |
| Finder R. | 10B |
| Deegan D. | 11D |

(c)

| Smokers | Non-smokers |
|---|---|
| Greg | Alice |
| Mary | June |
| Jenny | Peter |

(d)

| Model | Manufacturer |
|---|---|
| Pajero | Mitsubishi |
| Lancer | Mitsubishi |
| Patrol | Nissan |
| Statesman | Holden |

(e)

| Name | Age | House |
|------|-----|-------|
| Green H. | 17 | Henderson |
| Rich R. | 16 | Henderson |
| Davis G. | 17 | Radcliffe |

# Significant output reports

Binary relationships are the most common type of facts. As much information as possible should be expressed as binary relationships. Even situations that can be expressed as unary relations are often converted to binary relationships by introducing a new entity. For example:

| Drinker | Non-drinker |
|---------|-------------|
| Mary | Alan |
| Rudy | Michelle |
| Robin | Gary |

could be represented as:

   Person (Name) 'Mary' drinks

   Person (Name) 'Alan' is a non-drinker

or as follows:

| Person | Drinker |
|--------|---------|
| Mary | Y |
| Rudy | Y |
| Robin | Y |
| Alan | N |
| Michelle | N |
| Gary | N |

This can then be represented as:

   Person (Name) 'Mary' has Drinker (Code) 'Y'

This new representation shows how the two unary relationships (drinks, is a non-drinker) have been converted into a binary relationship. This is frequently more efficient to implement when converting a conceptual schema to logical and internal schema and is the preferred method of representation.

Step one of the conceptual design process could be thought of as representing as much of the universe of discourse as possible as binary relationships. Higher order arities are used only when information is lost if binary relationships are used. Consider the following situation:

| Name | Subject | Grade |
|------|---------|-------|
| Black H. | English | A |
| Grey R. | Mathematics | C |
| Brown G. | English | B |

This situation could be represented as:

Student (Name) 'Black H.' studies Subject (Name) 'English'

Student (Name) 'Black H.' obtained Grade (Code) 'A'

The data supplied suggests that each student studied only one subject and received only one grade. In this case the linkage through the student's name implies the relationship between the Subject and the Grade, that is, Black H. only studied English, Black H. received an A, therefore the A was for English. But what if this is not the case? The following table may better represent the true situation.

| Name | Subject | Grade |
|------|---------|-------|
| Black H. | English | A |
| | Mathematics | C |
| | Science | B |
| Grey R. | English | A |
| | Mathematics | C |
| | History | D |
| Brown G. | English | B |
| | Mathematics | D |
| | Geography | A |

In this situation, the binary relationships:

Student (Name) 'Black H.' studies Subject (Name) 'English'

Student (Name) 'Black H.' obtained Grade (Code) 'A'

would lose information because the A could apply to the subjects Mathematics or Science, which are also studied by Black H. This situation would have to be represented with the ternary relationship:

Student (Name) 'Black H.' in Subject (Name) 'English' obtained Grade (Code) 'A'

When choosing to represent information using ternary (and higher arity) relationships, there must be examples within the data that show information is lost if binaries are used. Repetition and blanks in output reports are indicators that there *may* be relationships other than binary. Output reports that contain sufficient data to demonstrate all relationships are called **significant output reports**. If the designer is supplied with output reports that are not significant some **assumptions** may have to be made. These assumptions should be noted at design time and checked with the universe of discourse expert before the conceptual schema is completed.

## EXERCISE 4

### Question 1
Write elementary facts that express the following unary relationships as binary.
(a) Person (Name) 'Mandy' is a believer
Person (Name) 'Gerry' is a non-believer
(b) Person (Name) 'Cassy' is female
Person (Name) 'Jim' is male
(c) Person (Name) 'Graham' is employed
Person (Name) 'Malcolm' is unemployed

### Question 2
Write elementary facts for each of the following significant output reports.

(a)

| Name | Phone | Suburb |
|------|-------|--------|
| Gary | 33452321 | Sunnybank |
| Jenny | 33450691 | Sunnybank |
| James | 32661499 | Nundah |
| April | 38081234 | Inala |

(b)

| Name | Suburb | Postcode |
|------|--------|----------|
| David | Clayfield | 4011 |
| Harry | Sunnybank | 4109 |
| Karen | Bagot | 0820 |
| Mary | Zeehan | 7469 |
| Noel | Clayfield | 4011 |
| Stephen | Sunnybank | 4109 |

(c)

| Car | Cylinders | Towing capacity |
|-----|-----------|-----------------|
| Commodore | 4 | 1.2 tonnes |
| | 6 | 1.5 tonnes |
| | 8 | 2.0 tonnes |
| Pajero | 4 | 1.5 tonnes |
| | 6 | 2.0 tonnes |
| Pintara | 4 | 1.2 tonnes |

(d)

| Language | Author | Year |
|----------|--------|------|
| Pascal | Wirth | 1971 |
| Prolog | Roussel | 1972 |
| Modula 2 | Wirth | 1979 |

(e)

| Author | Book | Price ($) |
|--------|------|-----------|
| Allen Y. | The Last Return | 19.95 |
| | The Lost City | 25.95 |
| Baker T. | The Last Return | 19.95 |

(f)

| Student | Event | Place |
|---------|-------|-------|
| Jemma | 100 metres | 1 |
| Mary | 100 metres | 2 |
| Joan | 100 metres | 3 |
| Mary | 200 metres | 1 |
| Andrea | 200 metres | 2 |
| Jemma | 200 metres | 3 |

(g)

| Student | Semester | Subject | Rating |
|---------|----------|---------|--------|
| Jones A. | 1 | English | A |
| | 2 | English | B |
| | 1 | History | C |
| | 2 | History | A |
| Green W. | 1 | English | B |
| | 2 | English | C |
| | 1 | Geography | A |
| | 2 | Geography | C |

(h)

| Race | Track | Winner | Owner |
|------|-------|--------|-------|
| 1 | Eagle Farm | Grey Synd | Brown T. |
| 2 | Eagle Farm | Tom Boy | Grey O. |
| 3 | Eagle Farm | Fourlap | Green F. |
| 1 | Sandown | Girrop | Black Y. |
| 2 | Sandown | Grey Synd | Brown T. |

(i)

| ISBN | Title | Authors | No. pages |
|------|-------|---------|-----------|
| 0 07 470032 4 | New Senior Computer Studies | Mark Baker Neil Frost | 252 |
| 0 07 470097 9 | Information Processing and Management | Mark Scott John Holland | 288 |
| 0 07 470250 5 | Chemistry Laboratory Manual | Mark Gould | 208 |

(j)

| Company | Item | Quantity |
|---------|------|----------|
| Software Galore | Word Maker | 25 |
| | Sum Worker | 50 |
| | Battle Star | 100 |
| Narvey Horman | Rose 2 4 6 | 50 |
| | Battle Star | 25 |

(k)  The Smith family tree consists of:

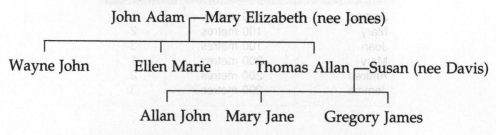

(l)

| Mare's name | Price ($) | Stallion's name | Price ($) |
|-------------|-----------|-----------------|-----------|
| Anna Dane | 120 000 | Grey Synd | 100 000 |
| New Blood | 20 000 | Big Star | 120 000 |
| | | Green Door | 50 000 |

(m) We wish to store the results of the primary school sports day on computer. The day consists of ten events, each with a unique name such as '50 metre sprint'. Each student in the school belongs to one of the six houses. Each house has one student in each event for each year level (Year 1 to Year 7). For each student, we wish to record the events they entered and the places gained. We wish to be able to obtain the number of times each house gained each place so that we can allocate the trophies.

(n)

| Student | Form | Form room | Teacher |
|---------|------|-----------|---------|
| Jones B. | 11B | 204 | Glead Y. |
| Green S. | 12A | 105 | Flounder T. |
| Hanson H. | 11B | 204 | Glead Y. |
| Brown R. | 10C | 120 | Flynn T. |
| Hashom P. | 12A | 105 | Flounder T. |

## STEP ②

# Draw the fact types

The second step in the conceptual schema design process is to draw a graphical representation of the facts obtained in the first step. Elementary facts contain entity types, reference schemes and roles. An entity type is represented by a named ellipse drawn with a full line. Reference schemes are represented by named ellipses drawn with a dotted line. Roles are represented by rectangles and relationships are shown by lines joining the elements of the relationship.

**Entity**

**Reference scheme**

**Role**

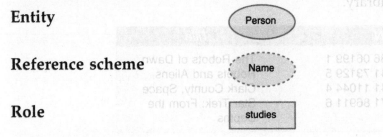

The elementary fact:

Student (First Name) 'Mary' studies/is studied by Subject (Name) 'English' would be represented by:

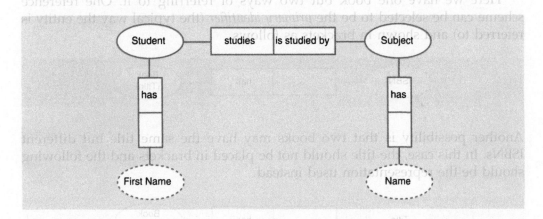

This diagram explicitly shows the reference schemes for the entities. If the values used in referring to the entities correspond exactly (i.e. for each entity there is a unique value) then this diagram may be expressed in a more concise form. The reference scheme can be placed in brackets near the entity type name as follows.

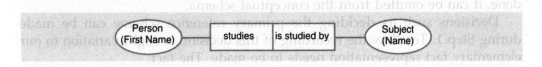

As before with the elementary facts, the reverse role can be implied, thus reducing the schema to the following.

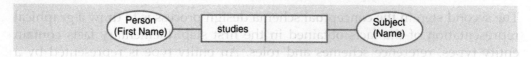

However, there are still times when the dotted ellipse will be used. It is necessary when an entity has more than one reference scheme. Consider the following report for a library.

| ISBN | Title |
| --- | --- |
| 0 586 06199 1 | The Robots of Dawn |
| 0 441 73129 5 | Robots and Aliens |
| 0 441 11044 4 | Clark County, Space |
| 0 671 86911 6 | Star Trek: From the Depths |

The elementary fact from this report would be:
    Book (ISBN) '0 586 06199 1' is Book (Title) 'The Robots of Dawn'
    Here we have one book but two ways of referring to it. One reference scheme can be selected to be the *primary identifier* (the typical way the entity is referred to) and shown in brackets as follows.

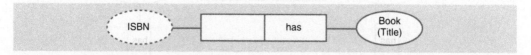

Another possibility is that two books may have the same title but different ISBNs. In this case, the title should not be placed in brackets and the following should be the representation used instead.

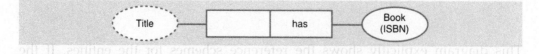

    *Assumption*—More than one book can have the same title
**Note** the inclusion of the assumption. This is an assumption by the designer because this rule is not demonstrated in the data supplied in the report. This assumption should be verified by the universe of discourse expert. Once this is done, it can be omitted from the conceptual schema.
    Decisions such as deciding the primary reference scheme can be made during Step 1. To allow the recording of this decision, a slight variation to our elementary fact representation needs to be made. The fact:

Book (ISBN) '0 586 06199 1' is Book (Title) 'The Robots of Dawn' seems to imply there are two entities of the same type that have some relationship. This is not the case; it is one entity with two reference schemes. To stop the confusion, the second occurrence of the entity can be removed as follows:

Book (ISBN) '0 586 06199 1' has (Title) 'The Robots of Dawn'

This representation clearly shows we have one entity with two ways of referring to it and it corresponds with the diagram.

It is possible to have two entities of the same type having a relationship. For example:

Person (Name) 'Jane' employs Person (Name) 'Greg'

This situation is drawn using a ring fact type as shown below.

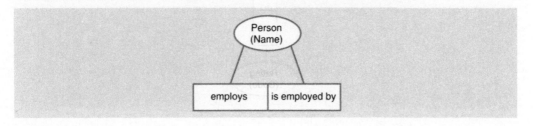

The reverse role has been included here only for clarity, to show how the ring fact is to be read.

# Ternary facts

Representing ternary relationships is a logical extension of our current model. For example:

Student (Name) 'Black H.' in Subject (Name) 'English' obtained Grade (Code) 'A'

would be represented as:

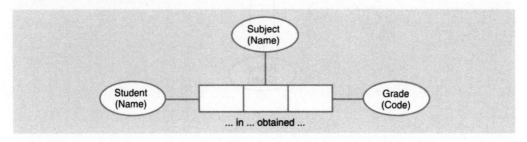

This representation has some limitations (not discussed here) and so is not used here. An alternative representation called a nesting will be used. Nesting considers a relationship between two entities to be an entity itself, called a **nested entity type**. In the above example the student and the subject could be combined into a nested entity type. The nested entity type is shown on the conceptual schema diagram as an ellipse round the roles connecting the two entities. The previous ternary fact type would be represented in nested form as follows:

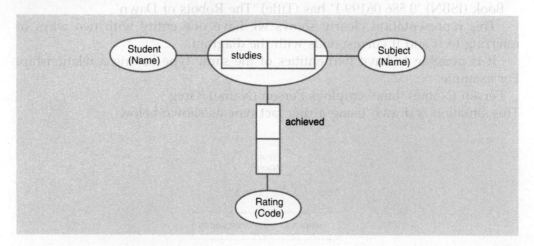

The nested entity type can be named. This is useful when referring to the nested entity type in later steps of the procedure. In the previous example the nested entity type could be called 'Enrolment'. The schema would then appear as follows:

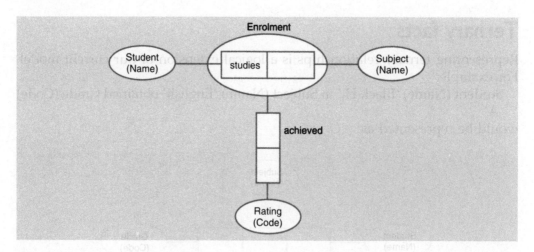

# Multiple fact types

When a universe of discourse contains more than one elementary fact, conceptual schema is formed by drawing the facts without repeating entities. That is, if an entity type is contained in two elementary facts then one ellipse will be drawn with two lines leading to roles. For example, consider the following report:

| Title | Author | Cost ($) |
|---|---|---|
| The Robots of Dawn | Isaac Asimov | 13.25 |
| Robots and Aliens | Isaac Asimov | 18.95 |
| Clark County, Space | Allen Steele | 13.25 |
| Star Trek: From the Depths | Victor Milan | 10.50 |

Valid elementary facts from this report would be:

Book (Title) 'The Robots of Dawn' is written by Author (Name) 'Isaac Asimov'

Book (Title) 'The Robots of Dawn' costs Amount ($) 13.25

The schema for these facts would be:

The entity type Book appears in both sentences but only one ellipse is drawn representing this entity type. This ellipse is then joined by a line to the two roles from the two elementary facts. It is not necessary to retain the order of the entity types in the sentences across the diagram. The diagrammatic representations can be read in either direction. Where an entity type plays a number of roles the diagrams can get quite cluttered. Diagrams should always be laid out as clearly as possible. The following diagram shows another representation for the same elementary sentences.

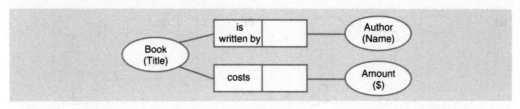

Ellipses for nested entity types are also drawn only once. For example the elementary facts:

Student (Name) 'Black H.' in Subject (Name) 'English' obtained Grade (Code) 'A'

Student (Name) 'Black H.' in Subject (Name) 'English' is taught by Teacher (Name) 'Green T.'

would be shown as follows:

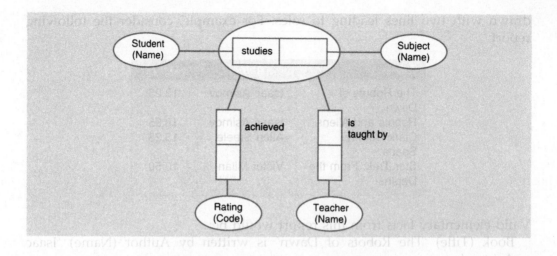

## EXERCISE ⑤

### Question 1

Which of the following are valid conceptual schema diagrams given that suitable names can be supplied?

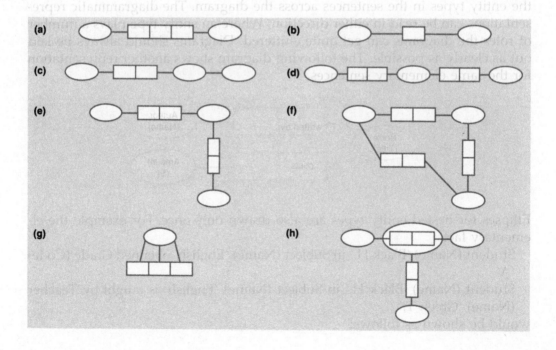

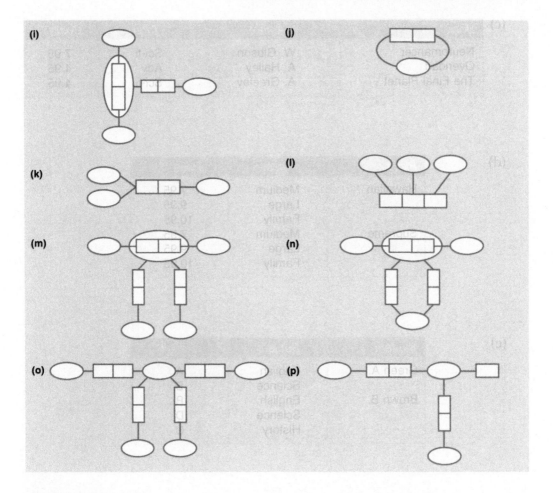

## Question 2

Draw conceptual schema diagrams for the following output reports (i.e. perform Steps 1 and 2 of the conceptual schema design procedure).

(a)

| Person | Age |
|--------|-----|
| Mary Smith | 42 |
| Alan Brown | 36 |
| Neil Green | 24 |

(b)

| Person | Height (cm) | Weight (kg) |
|--------|-------------|-------------|
| Green G. | 170 | 65 |
| Brown B. | 180 | 70 |
| Grey G. | 120 | 40 |
| Black B. | 200 | 90 |

(c)

| Book | Author | Type | Cost ($) |
|------|--------|------|----------|
| Neuromancer | W. Gibson | Sci-fi. | 7.95 |
| Overload | A. Hailey | Adv. | 4.95 |
| The Final Planet | A. Greeley | Sci-fi. | 4.95 |

(d)

| Pizza | Size | Price ($) |
|-------|------|-----------|
| Hawaiian | Medium | 7.95 |
| | Large | 9.95 |
| | Family | 10.95 |
| Supreme | Medium | 7.95 |
| | Large | 9.95 |
| | Family | 10.95 |

(e)

| Student | Subject | Result |
|---------|---------|--------|
| Green A. | English | A |
| | Science | B |
| Brown B. | English | B |
| | Science | D |
| | History | C |

(f)

| Pizza | Ham | Pineapple | Toppings Capsicum | Onion | Beef | Peperoni |
|-------|-----|-----------|----------|-------|------|----------|
| Hawaiian | ✓ | ✓ | | | | |
| Peperoni | | | | ✓ | ✓ | ✓ |
| Supreme | ✓ | ✓ | ✓ | ✓ | ✓ | ✓ |

(g)

| Student | Subject | Teacher | Room |
|---------|---------|---------|------|
| Brown B. | English | Davis M. | E101 |
| Green T. | English | Hoover E. | E101 |
| Grey D. | English | Davis M. | E101 |
| Brown B. | Science | Gribble T. | S102 |
| Green T. | Science | Hanner G. | S102 |
| Grey D. | Science | Hanner G. | S102 |

(h)

| Year level | Subject | Day | Lesson |
|---|---|---|---|
| 12 | English | Monday | 1 |
| | | Tuesday | 6 |
| | | Thursday | 3 |
| | History | Monday | 3 |
| | | Wednesday | 2 |
| | | Friday | 4 |
| 11 | English | Tuesday | 2 |
| | | Wednesday | 8 |
| | | Friday | 4 |
| | History | Monday | 1 |
| | | Tuesday | 3 |
| | | Friday | 7 |

(i) The corner store has a small video lending section. They wish to record the video transactions on a computer. For ease of data entry each customer is allocated a number when they borrow their first video. This number is recorded with the customer's name. Each video has been allocated a unique number to ease data entry. Each video can be borrowed for one week, so the date borrowed needs to be recorded.

(j)

| Item | RRP ($) | Price ($) | Discount ($) |
|---|---|---|---|
| Riders Jeans | 59.95 | 40.95 | 19.00 |
| Loader Tops | 32.95 | 20.00 | 12.95 |
| Jacky Howes | 12.95 | 12.95 | |
| Socks | | 3.50 | |

RRP—Recommended Retail Price

(k)

| Event no. | Age | Distance | Place | Time | Student | Points |
|---|---|---|---|---|---|---|
| 1 | 13 | 100 metres | 1 | 12.10 | A. Smith | 10 |
| | | | 2 | 12.21 | B. Green | 8 |
| | | | 3 | 12.30 | C. Black | 6 |
| 2 | 14 | 100 metres | 1 | 12.11 | G. Hannon | 10 |
| | | | 2 | 12.15 | B. Allan | 8 |
| | | | 3 | 12.18 | C. Caves | 6 |

(l)

| Teacher | Class | Room | Students |
|---|---|---|---|
| Green A. | 11ENG | 102 | 25 |
| Brown D. | 11ENG | 103 | 22 |
| Green A. | 12HIS | 201 | 13 |
| Brown D. | 9SCI | 103 | 28 |

(m)

| Model | Cylinders | Passengers | Doors |
|---|---|---|---|
| Super Wagon | 6 | 7 | 5 |
| Standard Wagon | 6 | 5 | 5 |
| Short Wheel Base | 4 | 2 | 3 |
| Troop Carrier | 6 | 10 | 3 |

(n)

| Suburb | Street | Number | Owner | Size (sq. m) |
|---|---|---|---|---|
| Clayfield | Barton | 12 | Smyth A. | 504 |
| | | 21 | Robertson Q. | 645 |
| | | 34 | Howes W. | 405 |
| | Grayson | 5 | Smyth A. | 840 |
| | | 12 | Grey T. | 645 |
| Nundah | Staid | 14 | Robertson Q. | 450 |
| | | 12 | Black T. | 780 |
| | Barton | 12 | Green H. | 560 |
| | | 17 | Kramer Q. | 970 |

# Population check

Once the first draft of the conceptual schema diagram is drawn (Step 2) a population check should be applied to ensure the diagram makes sense. Each fact should be checked by reading the diagram using at least one set of values supplied by the universe of discourse expert. The output report concerning parking for a particular company, outlined in the following table:

| Employee | Permit no. | Car |
|---|---|---|
| Gryner E. | 12345 | 123 ABC |
| Smythe T. | 12346 | 294 HAT |
| Earnshaw Y. | 12347 | 184 ESD |

resulted in the following conceptual schema after Steps 1 and 2 had been completed.

As a check, the designer should then read the following facts from the diagram:

Employee 'Gryner E.' drives Car '123 ABC'
Employee 'Gryner E.' holds Permit '12345'

Both these statements make sense and are consistent with the output report supplied. The possibility is high that the designer is correct. Remember the best judge of this is the universe of discourse expert. This process of reading the conceptual schema diagram is a useful tool when checking the conceptual schema with the universe of discourse expert.

A formal population check can also be performed. This involves entering *all* supplied values in tables under their appropriate roles. This population check can be useful later in the conceptual schema design procedure when decisions need to be made on constraints. The following diagram shows the formal population check applied to the previous example.

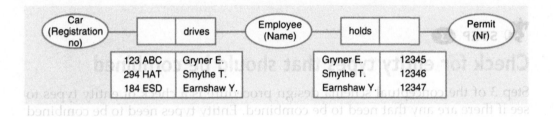

## EXERCISE 6

### Question 1

Apply the first two steps of the conceptual schema design procedure and apply a formal population check for each of the following significant output reports.

(a)

| Artist | Album |
|--------|-------|
| Celine Dion | Falling Into You |
| Don McLean | American Pie |
| Carole King | Tapestry |
| Jeff Buckley | Grace |

(b)

| Movie | Stars |
|-------|-------|
| The Truth about Cats and Dogs | Uma Thurman, Janeane Garofalo |
| Jerry Maguire | Tom Cruise |
| The Craft | Fairuza Balk, Robin Tunney, Neve Campbell |

(c)

| Colour | Stone | Hardness |
|--------|---------|----------|
| Yellow | Quartz | 7 |
| | Diamond | 10 |
| | Citrine | 7 |
| Green | Topaz | 8 |
| | Sapphire | 9 |
| | Diamond | 10 |
| Blue | Spinel | 8 |
| | Quartz | 7 |
| | Diamond | 10 |

 STEP ③

# Check for entity types that should be combined

Step 3 of the conceptual schema design procedure is a check of entity types to see if there are any that need to be combined. Entity types need to be combined for a variety of reasons. These reasons are detailed in the following examples. If one object is located in two (or more) entity types, entity types should be combined. Consider the following output report.

| Company | Manager | Owner |
|---------|---------|-------|
| Softserve Pty Ltd | Amie Boston | Graham Steel |
| Hardsell Pty Ltd | Graham Steel | Graham Steel |
| Macro Hard Pty Ltd | John Stephens | Mary McDonald |

Steps 1 and 2 yield:
  Company (Name) 'Softserve Pty Ltd' has Manager (Name) 'Amie Boston'
  Company (Name) 'Softserve Pty Ltd' has Owner (Name) 'Graham Steel'

Here the Manager and Owner are shown as separate entity types. The person Graham Steel plays the role of managing, as well as owning, a company. When one entity is a member of two entity types then these entity types should be combined. The above example would result in the following diagram when the entities Manager and Owner are combined.

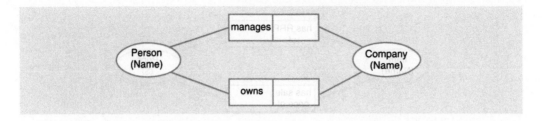

**Note:** The words used to label the roles now are very important as they convey the information formerly held in the entity type name. The following diagram would not be suitable because information pertaining to the positions of the people is lost.

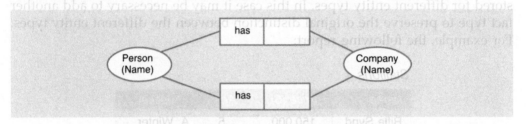

Entity types should also be combined if the different types are to be compared. That is, if entity types have the same unit and you may wish to add, subtract, multiply or divide them then the entity types should be combined. For example, the output report:

| Item | RRP ($) | Sale price ($) |
|------|---------|----------------|
| Blue Jeans | 59.95 | 40.95 |
| Shirts | 32.95 | 20.00 |
| Socks | 9.95 | 5.50 |

RRP—Recommended Retail Price

would result in the following conceptual schema diagram using Steps 1 and 2.

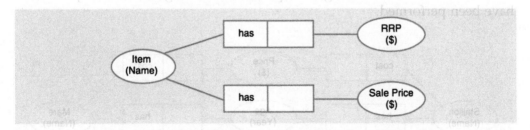

Here the recommended retail price and the sale price have the same units and you may wish to subtract the Sale Price from the RRP to obtain a discount. Combining these entity types would result in the following diagram.

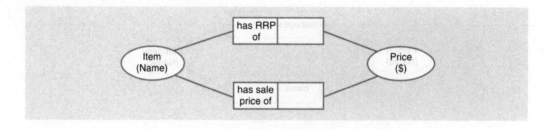

Again it is important to note that the naming of the roles becomes crucial to preserve the information regarding the types of prices in this example.

Entity types should also be combined when the same information is to be stored for different entity types. In this case it may be necessary to add another fact type to preserve the original distinction between the different entity types. For example, the following report:

### Stallions

| Name | Price ($) | Age | Jockey |
|------|-----------|-----|--------|
| Rifle Synd | 150 000 | 5 | A. Winter |
| Celcast | 50 000 | 12 | T. Spider |
| Know All | 120 000 | 8 | M. Whitaker |

### Mares

| Name | Price ($) | Age | Jockey |
|------|-----------|-----|--------|
| Elsie's Choice | 120 000 | 6 | M. Smith |
| Mary Jane | 20 000 | 3 | J. Jones |
| Top Notch | 90 000 | 5 | A. Winter |

would result in the following conceptual schema diagram after Steps 1 and 2 have been performed.

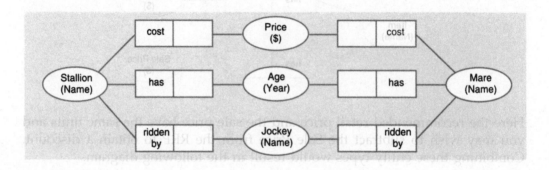

As we are storing the same information about the two entity types Stallion and Mare, Step 3 requires that these entity types be combined resulting in the following diagram.

**Note:** The original distinction between the types of horses cannot be preserved by the use of appropriate labels in the roles. A new entity type (Gender in this example) must be added to the diagram to retain the information contained in the original entity type names.

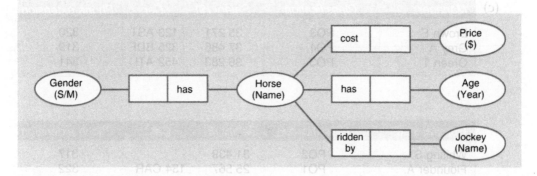

In summary, the third step of the conceptual schema design procedure requires the combining of entity types when:
(a) a particular entity can be a member of two entity types,
(b) entity types have the same unit and you may wish to add, subtract, multiply or divide them, or
(c) the same information is to be stored for the different entity types.

No information should be lost during this step. Information contained in the original entity type names can be retained by either changing the words used to describe roles (used in the first two situations) or adding an extra entity type (used in the third situation).

## EXERCISE 7

### Question 1
Perform Steps 1, 2 and 3 of the conceptual schema design procedure for the following output reports.

(a)

| Prime Minister | Born | Represented |
|---|---|---|
| Barton E. | NSW | NSW |
| Deakin A. | Vic. | Vic. |
| Fadden A. | Qld | Qld |
| Curtin J. | Vic. | WA |
| Hawke R. | WA | Vic. |

(b)

| Prime Minister | Born | Died |
|---|---|---|
| Barton E. | 1849 | 1920 |
| Deakin A. | 1856 | 1919 |
| Watson J. | 1867 | 1941 |
| Reid G. | 1845 | 1918 |
| Fisher A. | 1862 | 1952 |

(c)

| Manager | Classification | Salary ($) | Car | Phone extension |
|---|---|---|---|---|
| Brown E. | PO3 | 35 271 | 123 AST | 320 |
| Grey A. | PO4 | 37 486 | 325 BDF | 319 |
| Green T. | PO3 | 36 283 | 452 ATI | 341 |

| General staff | Classification | Salary ($) | Car | Phone extension |
|---|---|---|---|---|
| Whiting S. | PO2 | 31 439 | - | 317 |
| Flounder A. | PO1 | 25 567 | 134 CAR | 322 |
| Salamander R. | PO2 | 29 235 | 975 AMT | 317 |
| Snapper Y. | PO1 | 25 567 | - | 345 |

(d)

| Employee | Department | Salary ($) | Budget ($) |
|---|---|---|---|
| Langer W. | Administration | 35 234 | 23 685 |
| Walters T. | Manufacturing | 20 875 | 123 345 |
| Lewis K. | Public Relations | 32 456 | 13 687 |
| Brick W. | Administration | 37 237 | 10 395 |

(e)

| Item | Wholesale ($) | Retail ($) | Trade ($) |
|---|---|---|---|
| Scissors | 24.68 | 35.99 | 33.69 |
| Pins | 3.56 | 4.62 | 4.20 |
| Hooks | 1.78 | 2.15 | 2.05 |
| Ruler | 3.45 | 5.12 | 4.90 |

(f)

| Company | Manager | Contact | Phone no. |
|---|---|---|---|
| John's Computers | John Crook | John Crook | 2843 7642 |
| Mobile Service | Ellen Trent | Gary Heller | 4983 3934 |
| Al's Stationery | Alan Cox | Mary Wells | 8462 2373 |

(g)

| Student | Tutor | Subject |
|---------|-------|---------|
| Addams M. | Jones T. | English |
| Addams M. | Graham R. | Science |
| Johns W. | Jones T. | English |
| Graham R. | Jones T. | Geography |

 **STEP 4**

# Add uniqueness constraints and check arity of fact types

This and subsequent steps of the conceptual schema design procedure are largely concerned with constraints. Constraints are the rules that place restrictions on the storing and changing of data. Step 3 focuses on **uniqueness** constraints which restrict the way in which data is stored. They play an important role when the logical schema for the relational model is obtained from the conceptual schema. In this step, once the uniqueness constraints are added, checks are made to see if facts are of the correct arity. Specifically, nested facts are checked to see if they are elementary.

A uniqueness constraint restricts the number of times an entity can play a particular role. The constraint  each teacher teaches in at most one room', used previously, is an example of a uniqueness constraint. Restricting the number of times an entity plays a role is important in maintaining the integrity of the database by reducing redundancy. **Redundancy** occurs when an elementary fact is stored more than once. If a fact is stored more than once then each occurrence of the fact must be changed if the information contained in the elementary fact changes. This is a tedious and time-consuming task which opens the possibility of errors when data is changed. Unchanged facts, in this situation, will cause incorrect data to be stored. This is called an update anomaly. Obviously update anomalies (and therefore redundancy) are to be avoided when designing databases.

## Uniqueness constraints on unary fact types

Although unary fact types are rarely used, they are the simplest example of the application of uniqueness constraints, so they will be considered first. As part of a gymnasium database, it is required to record whether the clients smoke. The following facts are to be stored for a particular gym:

The Client (Name) 'Mary' smokes
The Client (Name) 'Billy' smokes

The Client (Name) 'John' smokes

The conceptual schema with sample population would be as follows:

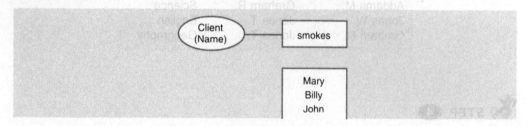

An attempt to add the fact:

The Client (Name) 'Billy' smokes

would result in the following:

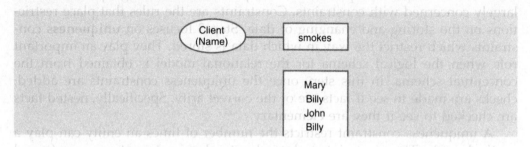

This now stores the fact 'Billy smokes' twice. As this is an unacceptable state for the database the addition would be rejected. There exists a uniqueness constraint that only allows the entity Client to play the role 'smokes' once. In other words, each client can only appear once in the population check. To record this uniqueness constraint on the conceptual schema an arrow-tipped bar is placed along the role, as shown in the following diagram.

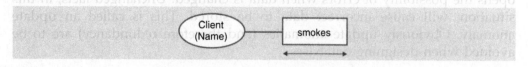

The bar may also be placed above the role as follows:

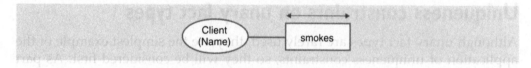

Since elementary facts are unique in a database, unary facts will always have a uniqueness constraint. In other words, whenever you have a unary fact type it will have a uniqueness constraint bar drawn along it.

# Uniqueness constraints on binary fact types

Binary fact types are more complicated with respect to uniqueness constraints. There are four possible different uniqueness constraints that are associated with a binary fact type. They are as follows:

(a) Consider the situation where students in a school are allocated to houses for sporting events. This situation would give the following schema:

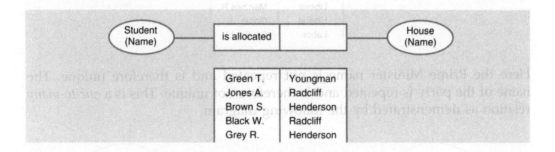

The populated schema shows that the students' names are not repeated but the house names are. Provided the sample population truly reflects the situation then no repetition of student names implies there is a uniqueness constraint on the role near the student entity. The repetition of the house names shows that there is no uniqueness constraint on the role near the house entity. That is, the student can play the role 'is allocated' only once but the house can play the reverse role 'is house of' a number of times. This can be shown diagrammatically below where a dot represents an entity.

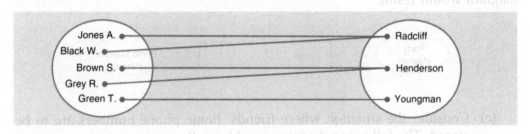

This diagram clearly shows why this is referred to as a *many-to-one* relation—many students are linked to one house. This type of relationship is represented using an arrowed bar over the unique role and nothing placed near the role which is not unique, as the following diagram shows.

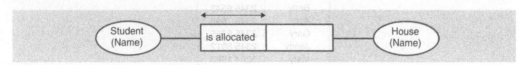

(b) Consider the situation where political party members have held the office of Prime Minister. This situation would give the following:

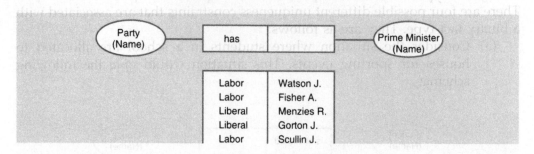

Here the Prime Minister name is not repeated and is therefore unique. The name of the party is repeated and is therefore not unique. This is a *one-to-many* relation as demonstrated by the following diagram.

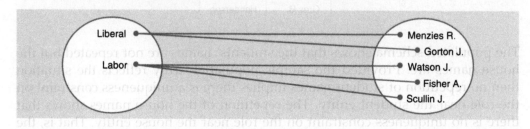

This, like the first example, is represented by putting the arrowed bar over the unique role, but this time it is the role on the right that is unique. The following diagram would result.

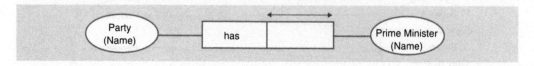

(c) Consider the situation where friends' home phone numbers are to be stored. The following diagram would result.

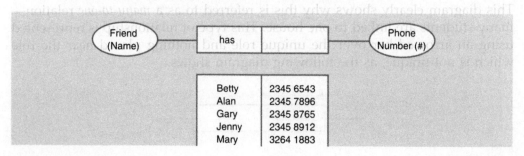

Here the friend's name is unique but so is the phone number, that is, neither a name nor a phone number are repeated. This is an example of a *one-to-one* relationship, as shown in the following diagram.

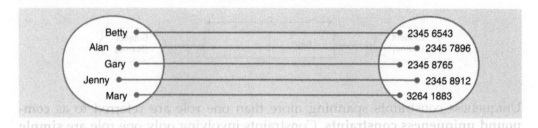

As before, this is represented on the diagram with an arrowed bar over the unique roles. In this case both roles will have bars, as in the following diagram.

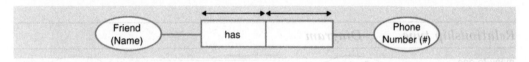

(d) Consider the situation where students study subjects. The following diagram would result.

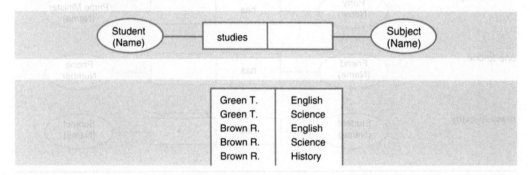

Neither the student nor the subject are unique, each is repeated in the population. Here only the combination of a particular student and a particular subject is unique. This is referred to as a *many-to-many* relation, as is shown in the following diagram.

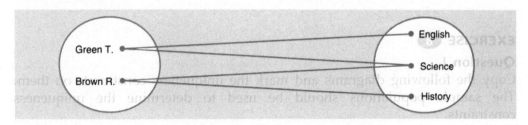

A many-to-many relation is represented by placing an arrowed bar across the unique combination of roles. In this case there are two roles to be spanned by the bar, as in the following diagram.

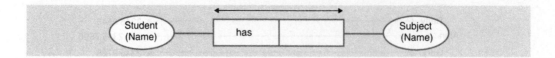

Uniqueness constraints spanning more than one role are referred to as **compound uniqueness constraints**. Constraints involving only one role are **simple uniqueness constraints**. The arrowheads on the uniqueness constraint bars can be omitted for unary and binary fact types. The following diagrams show the previous examples without arrowheads.

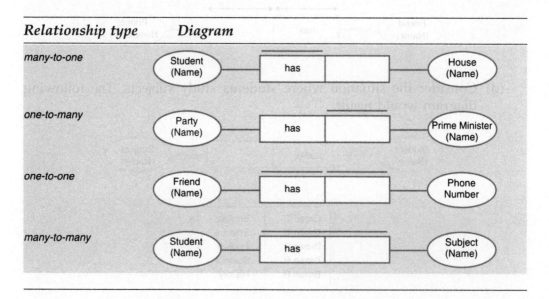

| *Relationship type* | *Diagram* |
|---|---|
| many-to-one | |
| one-to-many | |
| one-to-one | |
| many-to-many | |

When drawing schema and not using the arrowheads, care must be taken to make a clear distinction between the two separate bars of the one-to-one relationship and the one long bar used for the many-to-many relationship.

## EXERCISE 8

### Question 1

Copy the following diagrams and mark the uniqueness constraints on them. The sample populations should be used to determine the uniqueness constraints.

(a)

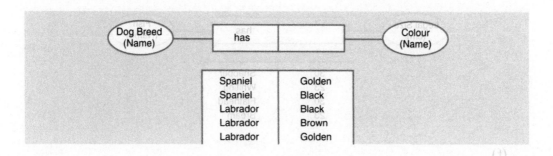

(b)

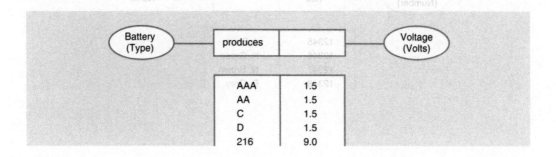

(c)

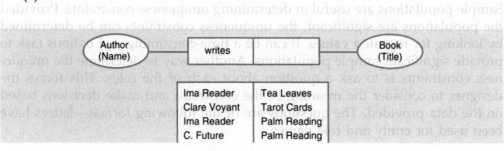

(d)

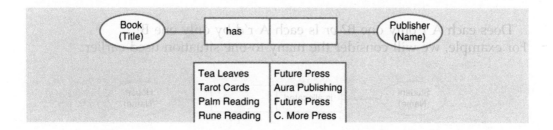

(e)

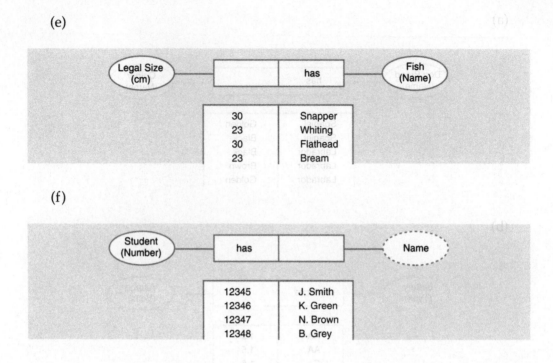

(f)

## Determining uniqueness constraints

Sample populations are useful in determining uniqueness constraints. Provided the populations are significant, the uniqueness constraints can be determined by looking for repeated values. It can be a time-consuming and tedious task to provide significant sample populations. Another way to determine the uniqueness constraints is to ask a question about each of the roles. This forces the designer to consider the meaning of the constraint and make decisions based on the data provided. The questions are of the following format—letters have been used for entity and role names.

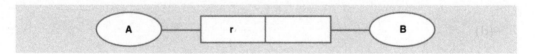

Does each A r only one B? *or* Is each A r'd by only one B?
For example, we will consider the many-to-one situation used earlier:

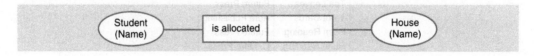

Does each Student have only one House allocated?
If the answer to the question is No, then nothing is done at this time. If the answer to the question is Yes, then a uniqueness constraint exists and a bar should be placed over the role being considered (that is, the role closest to the first entity in the sentence), as shown in the next example.

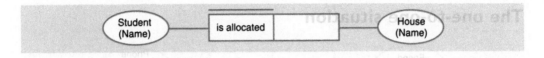

After one role has been considered, the question is asked for the reverse role. Which, in this case, gives the question:
Is each House allocated only one Student?
Again if the answer is Yes, then a bar would be placed over the role closest to House. But, as is the case here, if the answer is No, then no bar is placed over the role and the diagram remains as above.

The other three uniqueness constraint patterns for binary roles should also be examined. The remainder of the original examples used in the beginning of this section will be examined again using the questions to determine the uniqueness constraints. The answers to the questions can be found by examining the sample data. The diagrams will be repeated here to show the progressive steps. It is not necessary to redraw the schema each time a constraint is added. Simply add the constraint to the existing diagram.

## The one-to-many situation

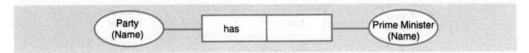

There are two questions to ask in this situation.

Question 1  Does each Party have only one Prime Minister?
Answer      No—both Labor and Liberal Parties have had more than one Prime Minister.

Therefore no constraint is to be added.

Question 2  Does each Prime Minister have only one Party?
Answer      Yes—no Prime Minister is shown to have more than one party.

A uniqueness constraint bar should be placed over the role closest to Prime Minister.

The one-to-many situation results in:

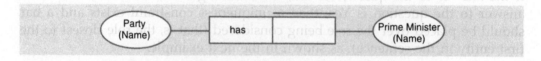

## The one-to-one situation

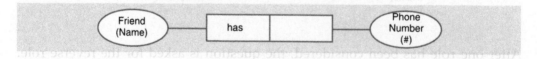

The two questions to ask in this situation are:

*Question 1*  Does each Friend have only one Phone Number?
*Answer*  Yes—no friend has two or more numbers in the example.

A uniqueness constraint bar should be placed over the role closest to Friend.

*Question 2*  Does each Phone Number have only one Friend?
*Answer*  Yes—no phone number belongs to more than one friend.

A uniqueness constraint bar should be placed over the role closest to Phone Number.

The one-to-one situation results in:

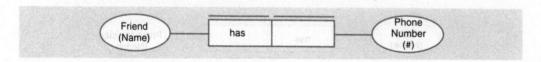

## The many-to-many situation

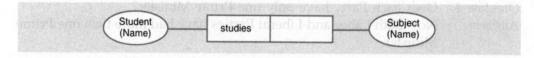

The two questions to ask for this situation are:

*Question 1*  Does each Student study only one Subject?
*Answer*  No—students study more than one subject.

Therefore no constraint is to be added.

*Question 2*  Is each Subject studied by only one Student?
*Answer*  No—subjects are studied by more than one student.

Since the answer to both questions has been 'No', the minimum uniqueness constraint covering both roles must be applied.

The many-to-many situation results in:

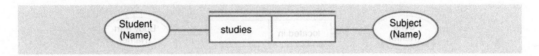

## EXERCISE 9

### Question 1

Copy the following diagrams and mark the uniqueness constraints on them. Use the questions to determine the uniqueness constraints. The data supplied should be considered significant and used to determine the constraints.

(a)

| Artist | Painting |
|---|---|
| Vincent van Gogh | The Potato Eaters |
| Gaustav Courbet | The Stonebreakers |
| Claude Monet | Gare Saint-Lazare |
| Edvard Munch | The Scream |
| Gaustav Courbet | The Burial at Ornans |

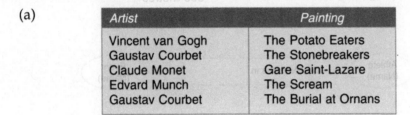

(b)     *Greek Gods*

| Name | Type |
|---|---|
| Amun | God of Thebes |
| Aten | Creator God |
| Atum | Sun God |
| Horus | Falcon God |
| Matt | Goddess of Truth |

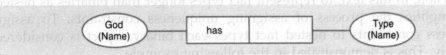

(c)

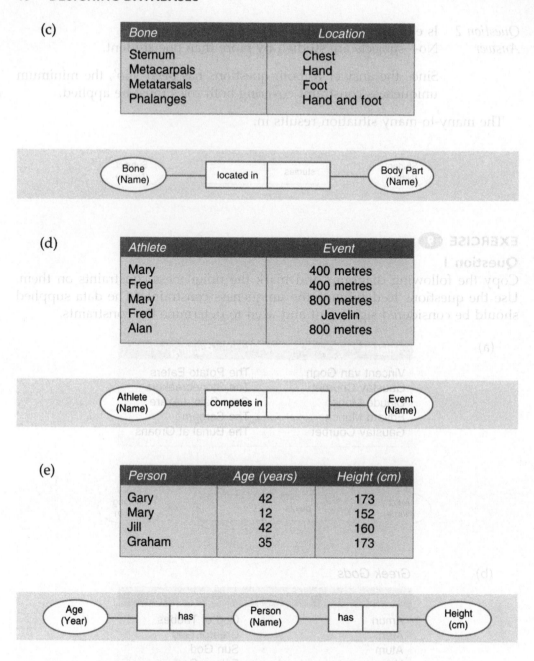

| Bone | Location |
| --- | --- |
| Sternum | Chest |
| Metacarpals | Hand |
| Metatarsals | Foot |
| Phalanges | Hand and foot |

Bone (Name) — located in — Body Part (Name)

(d)

| Athlete | Event |
| --- | --- |
| Mary | 400 metres |
| Fred | 400 metres |
| Mary | 800 metres |
| Fred | Javelin |
| Alan | 800 metres |

Athlete (Name) — competes in — Event (Name)

(e)

| Person | Age (years) | Height (cm) |
| --- | --- | --- |
| Gary | 42 | 173 |
| Mary | 12 | 152 |
| Jill | 42 | 160 |
| Graham | 35 | 173 |

Age (Year) — has — Person (Name) — has — Height (cm)

# Uniqueness constraints on longer fact types

The decision, in this text, to represent fact types longer than binaries as nested facts simplifies the process of assigning uniqueness constraints. To assign uniqueness constraints to nested fact types each binary aspect is considered separately. This is demonstrated in the following example.

*Output report*

| Student | Subject | Result |
|---------|---------|--------|
| Addams M. | English | A |
| Addams M. | Science | B |
| Johns W. | English | B |
| Graham R. | English | C |

*Schema*

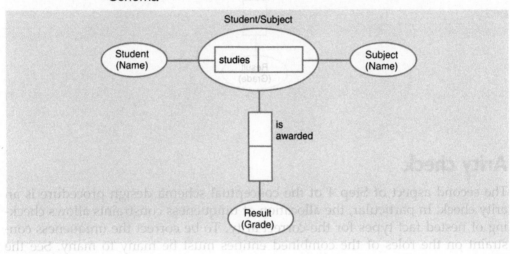

## Questions:

*Question 1* Does each Student study only one Subject?
*Answer* No.

*Question 2* Is each Subject studied by only one Student?
*Answer* No.

Therefore a uniqueness constraint bar goes across both roles between Student and Subject.

*Question 3* Is each Student/Subject awarded only one Result?
*Answer* Yes.

A uniqueness constraint bar is placed over the role closest to Student/Subject.

*Question 4* Is each Result awarded to only one Student/Subject?
*Answer* No.

The following example is thus produced.

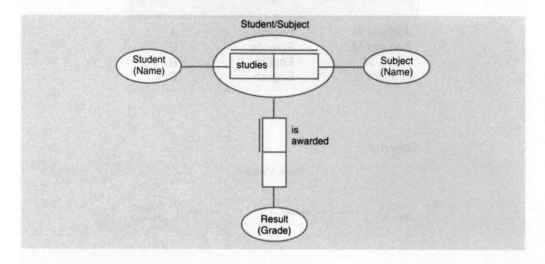

## Arity check

The second aspect of Step 4 of the conceptual schema design procedure is an arity check. In particular, the allocation of uniqueness constraints allows checking of nested fact types for the correct arity. To be correct the uniqueness constraint on the roles of the combined entities must be many to many. See the following figures.

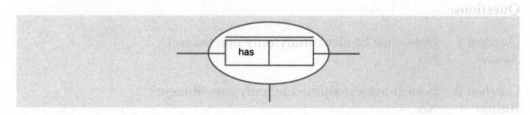

This type of situation has the correct arity.

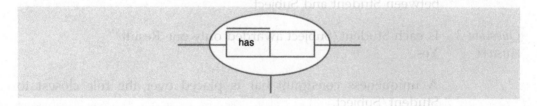

This type of situation is *not correct* and this nesting can be split into two elementary facts.

| Student | Room | Subject |
|---------|------|---------|
| Addams M. | 12 | English |
| Graham R. | 15 | English |
| Johns W. | 12 | English |
| Addams M. | 12 | Science |
| Graham R. | 15 | Science |
| Johns W. | 12 | Science |

This table could be (incorrectly) interpreted as:
Student (Name) 'Addams M.' in Room (#) 12 studies Subject (Name) 'English'
Steps 1, 2 and 3 would produce:

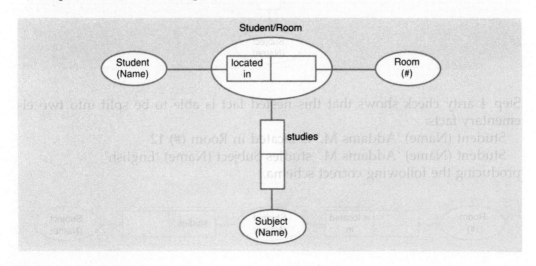

**Step 4 questions:**

*Question 1*   Is each Student located in only one Room?
*Answer*   Yes.

A uniqueness constraint bar should be placed over the role closest to Student.

*Question 2*   Does each Room have only one Student?
*Answer*   No.

*Question 3*   Does each Student/Room study only one Subject?
*Answer*   No.

*Question 4*   Is each Subject studied by only one Student/Room?
*Answer*   No.

A uniqueness constraint bar should be placed over both roles between Student/Room and Subject.

These steps will produce the following schema:

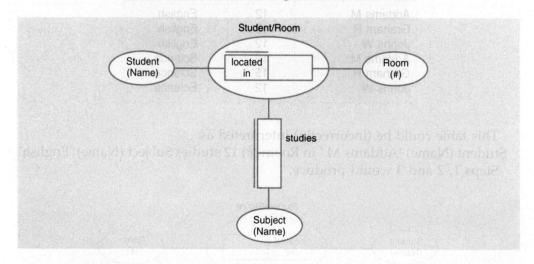

Step 4 arity check shows that this nested fact is able to be split into two elementary facts:

Student (Name) 'Addams M.' is located in Room (#) 12

Student (Name) 'Addams M.' studies Subject (Name) 'English'

producing the following correct schema.

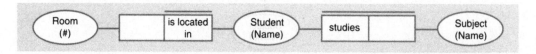

# Assumptions

The data contained in reports often does not *completely* describe the universe of discourse. This can lead to the data suggesting constraints that are not correct. In this case the database designer can make assumptions until such time as they can be validated by the domain expert. These assumptions must be stated explicitly on the schema. This is done by writing the heading 'Assumptions', and detailing, in English, the assumptions made. For example:

| Student | Gender |
| --- | --- |
| Addams M. | F |
| Graham R. | M |

Steps 1, 2 and 3 would produce:

Student (Name) 'Addams M.' has Gender (Code) 'F'

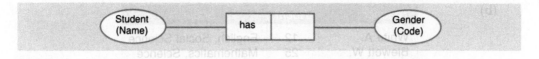

## Step 4

*Question 1*   Does each Student have only one Gender?
*Answer*       Yes.

A uniqueness constraint bar should be placed over the role closest to Student.

*Question 2*   Does each Gender have only one Student?
*Answer*       Yes (according to the data supplied).

Common sense and experience suggest that there will be more than one male or more than one female in the database. Therefore the designer may decide not to put a constraint on the role closest to Gender but instead make an assumption that reflects this.

This produces the following schema:

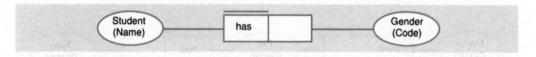

*Assumption*—Names of more than one person of a particular gender may be stored in the database.

## EXERCISE 10
### Question 1
Copy the following diagrams and mark the uniqueness constraints on them. Use the questions to determine the uniqueness constraints. The data supplied should be used to determine the answers.

(a)

| Student | Gender | Age |
|---------|--------|-----|
| Green M. | F | 14 |
| Grey R. | M | 15 |
| Black H. | F | 14 |
| Brown Q. | F | 14 |

(b)

| Teacher | Room | Subjects |
|---------|------|----------|
| White A. | 12 | English, Social Science |
| Blewett W. | 25 | Mathematics, Science |
| Ratray R. | 34 | English, Mathematics |

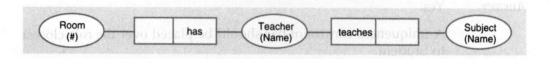

(c)

| Owner | Pet name | Type | Kennel no. |
|-------|----------|------|------------|
| Redman A. | Sky | Dog | 13 |
| Redman A. | Hook | Cat | 2 |
| Ranger L. | Silver | Dog | 24 |
| Pie T. | Silvester | Cat | 3 |

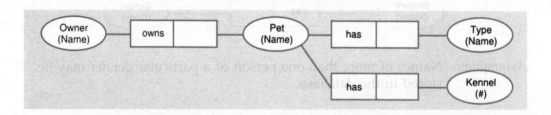

(d)

| Student | Year level | Boarder | Overseas | Scholarship |
|---------|------------|---------|----------|-------------|
| Ossenpheffer T. | 10 | Y | Y | N |
| Kracken J. | 12 | N | N | Y |
| King B. | 10 | N | Y | Y |
| Jack H. | 11 | Y | N | Y |

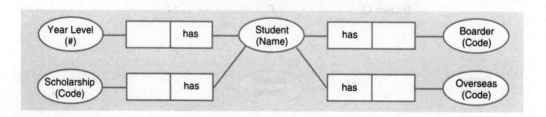

## Question 2

Perform Step 4 of the conceptual schema design procedure, including an arity check. Where necessary redraw the schema correctly, stating any assumptions if applicable.

(a)

| Teacher | Subject | Room |
|---------|---------|------|
| Green A. | Science | 12 |
| | Mathematics | 34 |
| | Form | 12 |
| Granger W. | English | 25 |
| | Geography | 25 |
| | Form | 25 |
| Dunn R. | English | 12 |

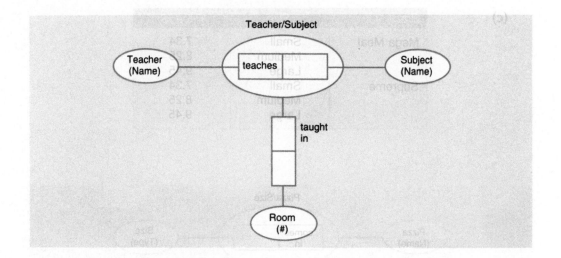

(b)

| Pet | Owner | Breed |
|-----|-------|-------|
| Rover | Brown J. | Spaniel |
| Fluff | Reed M. | Burmese |
| Spot | Brown J. | Dalmatian |
| Rover | Green H. | Terrier |
| Spot | Crane H. | Collie |

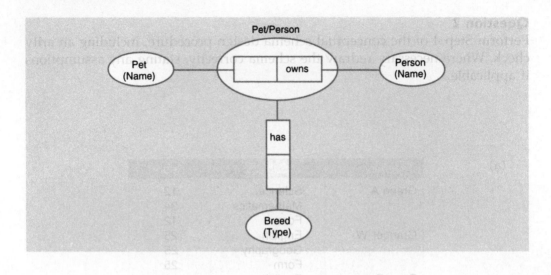

(c)

| Pizza | Size | Price ($) |
|-------|------|-----------|
| Mega Meat | Small | 7.34 |
| | Medium | 8.25 |
| | Large | 9.45 |
| Supreme | Small | 7.34 |
| | Medium | 8.25 |
| | Large | 9.45 |

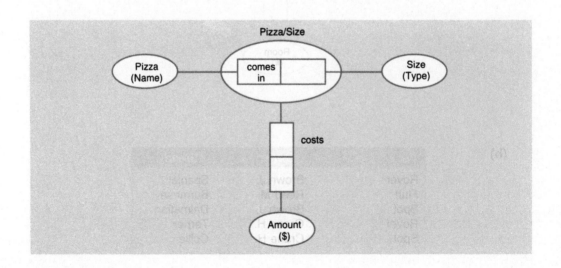

## Question 3

Perform Steps 1, 2, 3 and 4 of the conceptual schema design procedure for the following output reports.

(a)

| Prime Minister | Born | Represented |
|---|---|---|
| Barton E. | NSW | NSW |
| Deakin A. | Vic. | Vic. |
| Fadden A. | Qld | Qld |
| Curtin J. | Vic. | WA |
| Hawke R. | WA | Vic. |

(b)

| Prime Minister | Born | Died |
|---|---|---|
| Barton E. | 1849 | 1920 |
| Bruce S. | 1883 | 1967 |
| Curtin J. | 1885 | 1945 |
| Chifley B. | 1885 | 1951 |
| Holt H. | 1908 | 1967 |

(c)

| Student | Subject | Teacher | Room |
|---|---|---|---|
| Harrow W. | English | Watson | A24 |
| Harrow W. | Science | Richards | B34 |
| Harrow W. | Mathematics | Richards | B67 |
| Ayre R. | English | Richards | B13 |
| Ayre R. | Science | Graham | B34 |

(d)

| Employee | Department | Salary ($) | Budget ($) |
|---|---|---|---|
| Langer A. | Administration | 35 234 | 23 685 |
| Walters T. | Manufacturing | 20 875 | 123 345 |
| Lewis N. | Public Relations | 32 456 | 13 687 |
| Can T. | Administration | 20 875 | 13 687 |

(e)

| Person | Born | Died | Occupation |
|---|---|---|---|
| Kellerman Annette | 1886 | 1975 | Swimmer |
| Kelly Gene | 1822 | 1982 | Actor |
| Kelly Michael | 1850 | 1940 | Archbishop |
| Kelly Ned | 1855 | 1880 | Bushranger |
| Kelly Paul | 1955 | | Singer |
| Kmit Michael | 1910 | 1981 | Painter |

(f)

| Company | Manager | Phone number |
|---|---|---|
| John's Computers | John Crook | 2843 7642 |
| Mobile Service | Ellen Trent | 4983 3934 |
| Al's Stationery | Alan Cox | 8462 2373 |

(g)

| Drink | Size | Price ($) |
|---|---|---|
| Sars | 375 mL | 0.89 |
| | 1 litre | 1.30 |
| Lemonade | 375 mL | 0.85 |
| | 1 litre | 1.25 |
| Cola | 375 mL | 0.85 |
| | 600 mL | 1.25 |

# External uniqueness constraints

So far we have only considered uniqueness constraints involving one or more roles of the one fact type, but uniqueness constraints can involve roles from different fact types. Consider the following example where modern technology has eliminated the need to consider tied places.

| Event | Place | Athlete |
|---|---|---|
| 100 metres | 1 | Green T. |
| 100 metres | 2 | Grey H. |
| 100 metres | 3 | Brown G. |
| 200 metres | 1 | Black M. |
| 200 metres | 2 | Green T. |

This example would produce the following:

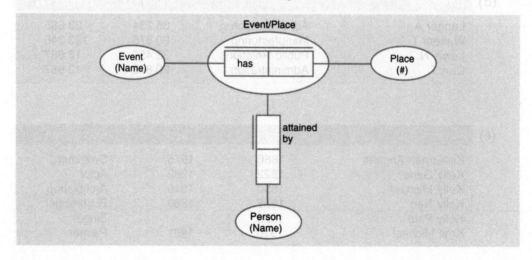

Let us consider the addition to the database of the following piece of information:

| Event | Place | Athlete |
|-------|-------|---------|
| 200 metres | 3 | Black M. |

This would not contravene our uniqueness constraints on our schema, but is obviously incorrect as it attempts to award both first and third place to the same athlete. There also exists a uniqueness constraint between the event and the athlete, that is, an athlete can only perform once in a particular event. This constraint is shown by joining the relevant role boxes by a dotted line to a circled 'u' as shown below. The 'u' stands for unique.

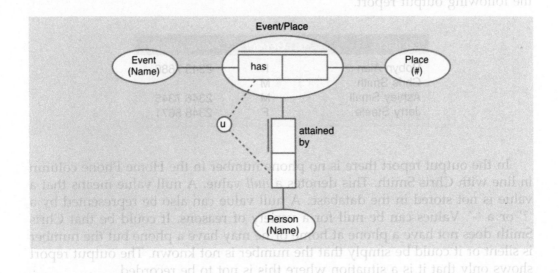

## EXERCISE 11

### Question 1

Perform the first four steps of the conceptual schema design procedure for the following output reports.

(a)

| Student | Tutor | Subject |
|---------|-------|---------|
| Adams P. | Jones T. | English |
| Adams P. | Green R. | Science |
| James W. | Jones T. | English |
| Graham R. | Jones T. | History |

(b)

| Student | Subject | Place |
|---------|---------|-------|
| Harold Y. | English | 1 |
| Barry P. | English | 2 |
| James W. | Geography | 1 |
| Harold Y. | Geography | 2 |
| Collins F. | Mathematics | 1 |

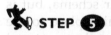 STEP 5

# Add mandatory constraints

Mandatory role constraints indicate which roles must be played by all entities of an entity type. Roles without mandatory constraints are optional. Consider the following output report.

| Contact | Gender | Home phone |
|---------|--------|------------|
| Robyn Alan | F | 2345 7686 |
| Chris Smith | M | |
| Ashley Small | M | 2346 7345 |
| Jerry Steele | F | 2348 5671 |

In the output report there is no phone number in the Home Phone column in line with Chris Smith. This denotes a *null* value. A null value means that a value is not stored in the database. A null value can also be represented by a '?' or a '-'. Values can be null for a variety of reasons. It could be that Chris Smith does not have a phone at home or he may have a phone but the number is silent or it could be simply that the number is not known. The output report shows only that it is a situation where this is not to be recorded.

On the previous report the first four steps of the conceptual schema design procedure would produce the following:

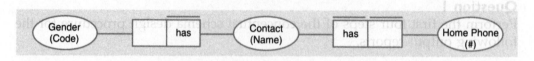

Step 5 requires that the role played by all entities of a particular entity type be identified. In the above situation it appears from the data supplied that the gender is to be recorded for every contact in the database. To show that all Contacts must have a Gender recorded, a mandatory role dot is placed where the line from the role meets the entity type as shown below.

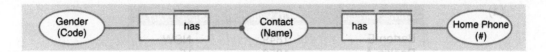

As in the case of the uniqueness constraint, the existence of a mandatory role constraint can be ascertained by finding the answer to a specific question. For the general case:

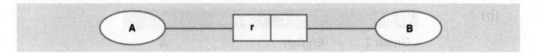

the question would be:

Does every A r a B? *or* Is every A r'd by a B?

The response to the answers of the questions is straightforward for mandatory roles. If the answer to the question is Yes, then a mandatory role dot is placed on the first entity type in the question where the line from the role being considered meets that entity type. If the answer is No, then nothing is done.

The questions for the above situation would be:

*Question 1*  Does every Contact have a Gender?
*Answer*     Yes (considered before).

A mandatory role dot is placed on Contact.

*Question 2*  Is every Gender a gender of a Contact?
*Answer*     Yes.

A mandatory role dot is placed on Gender.

*Question 3*  Does every Contact have a Home Phone?
*Answer*     No (Chris Smith's Home Phone is null).

*Question 4*  Is every Home Phone a number of a Contact?
*Answer*     Yes.

A mandatory role dot is placed on Home Phone.

This would result in the following updated diagram:

## EXERCISE 12

**Question 1**

Perform the first five steps of the conceptual schema design procedure on the following output reports.

(a)

| Prime Minister | Birth year | State born |
| --- | --- | --- |
| Barton E. | 1849 | NSW |
| Deakin A. | 1856 | Vic. |
| Watson J. | 1867 | ? |
| Reid G. | 1845 | ? |
| Curtin J. | 1885 | Vic. |
| Chifley J. | 1885 | NSW |

(b)

| Student | Subject | Semester | Result |
| --- | --- | --- | --- |
| Green T. | English | 1 | A |
|  |  | 2 | - |
|  | Science | 1 | B |
|  |  | 2 | - |
| Alan F. | English | 1 | B |
|  |  | 2 | - |
|  | Science | 1 | C |
|  |  | 2 | - |

(c)

| Prime Minister | Death age | Wife's name |
| --- | --- | --- |
| Forde F. | 93 | O'Reilly V. |
| Chifley J. | 66 | ? |
| Fraser J. | ? | Beggs T. |
| Hughes W. | 90 | Cutts E. |
| Hughes W. | 90 | Campbell M. |

(d)

| Room | Item | Number |
| --- | --- | --- |
| 12 | Chairs | 30 |
|  | Desks | 30 |
| 45 | Chairs | 45 |
|  | Desks | - |
| 67 | Chairs | 25 |
|  | Desks | 13 |

(e)

| Membership no. | Name | Date | Payment ($) |
| --- | --- | --- | --- |
| 12845 | Black T. | 12/03/97 | 12.00 |
|  |  | 15/03/97 | - |
|  |  | 18/03/97 | 24.00 |
| 14563 | Brown Y. | 12/03/97 | 14.00 |
|  |  | 16/03/97 | 12.00 |
|  |  | 19/03/97 | - |

# Disjunctive mandatory roles

Mandatory role constraints can involve more than one role. Consider the output reports below that describe the universe of discourse for the administration of a school.

### Employees

| Employee | Position | Department | Phone extension |
|----------|----------|------------|-----------------|
| Black R. | Principal | - | 234 |
| Brown G. | Deputy Principal | Administration | 235 |
| Grey H. | Deputy Principal | Administration | 237 |
| Green D. | Teacher | Secondary | 249 |
| White K. | Teacher | Secondary | 249 |
| Gold R. | Teacher | Primary | - |
| Magenta R. | Teacher | Primary | 257 |

### Duties

| Employee | Department managed |
|----------|--------------------|
| Black R. | Administration |
| Brown G. | Secondary |
| Grey H. | Primary |

The conceptual schema design procedure would produce the following:

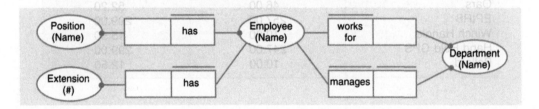

The above diagram does not show the constraint evident in the data that *every* employee either works for or manages a Department. This can be shown as follows:

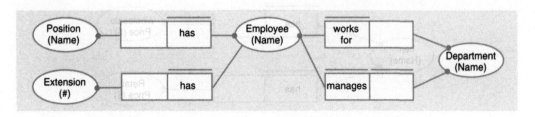

The mandatory constraint on the right of the Employee entity is a **disjunctive mandatory role** constraint. This constraint means that every employee works for or manages (or both) a Department. It can be difficult to draw the schema so that the lines from the roles meet in one point, so a disjunctive mandatory role constraint can also be shown using dotted lines, as shown in the following figure:

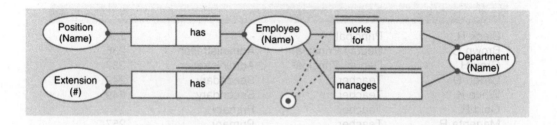

The first representation of the disjunctive mandatory role constraint is preferred as it produces less cluttered schema that are easier to read.

The use of a disjunctive should be considered when Step 3 of the conceptual schema design procedure identified entities that were combined. For example, consider the following output report on prices of items available from a chandlery store.

| Item | Wholesale price ($) | Retail price ($) |
|------|---------------------|------------------|
| Oars | 46.00 | 52.20 |
| EPIRB | 257.00 | 299.00 |
| Winch Handle | 10.00 | 15.50 |
| Hand Held GPS | 247.00 | 299.00 |
| Bollard | 10.00 | 12.50 |

The following schema would be produced if Step 3 (check for entities to be combined) is not performed.

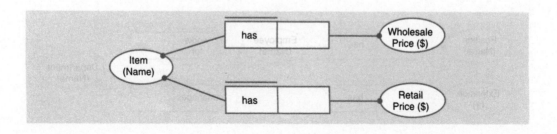

If Steps 1 to 4 are performed then the following schema would be produced:

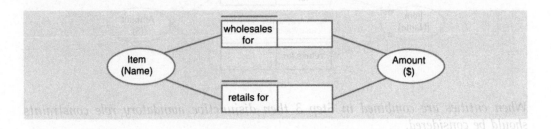

**Step 5 questions:**

*Question 1*   Does every Item wholesale for an Amount?
*Answer*       Yes.

               A mandatory role dot is placed on Item where the line from 'wholesales for' joins.

*Question 2*   Does every Item retail for an Amount?
*Answer*       Yes.

               A mandatory role dot is placed on Item where the line from 'retails for' joins.

*Question 3*   Is every Amount a wholesale price for an Item?
*Answer*       No (some are retail prices).

*Question 4*   Is every Amount a retail price for an Item?
*Answer*       No (some are wholesale prices).

This will produce the following schema:

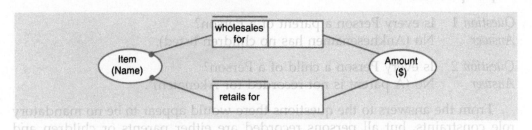

The Amounts, though, consist only of wholesale and retail prices as this entity came about from combining the entities Wholesale Price and Retail Price, each of which is mandatory (as shown in the non-combined schema previously). Therefore, a disjunctive mandatory role constraint exists for Amount for the roles 'wholesales for' and 'retails for' as shown in the diagram following.

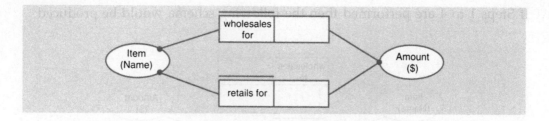

When entities are combined in Step 3 then disjunctive mandatory role constraints should be considered.

Disjunctive mandatory role constraints are also often associated with ring binary roles as in the following example which shows the parental relationships between Egyptian rulers.

| Parent | Child |
|--------|-------|
| Ay | Nefertiti |
| Nefertiti | Ankhesenamen |
| Akenaten | Ankhesenamen |
| Yuya | Ay |
| Tuya | Ay |

Steps 1 to 4 produce:

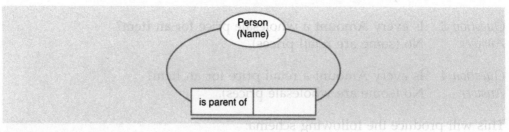

**Step 5 questions:**

*Question 1*   Is every Person a parent of a Person?
*Answer*       No (Ankhesenamen has no children listed).

*Question 2*   Is every Person a child of a Person?
*Answer*       No (A parent is not recorded for Akenaten)*.

From the answers to the questions there would appear to be no mandatory role constraints, but all persons recorded are either parents or children and

---

* It must be pointed out here that there is a distinction between what happens in the real world and what is recorded in databases. This particular question restated asks 'Does every child have a parent?' The answer to this question in the real world is obviously yes, but placing a mandatory role constraint on the 'is child of' role causes insurmountable problems when populating the database. Consider adding the first fact that Ay is the parent of Nefertiti. A mandatory role

therefore a disjunctive mandatory role constraint exists for Person for these two roles. This would be shown on the schema as follows:

## EXERCISE 13

## Question 1

Perform the first five steps of the conceptual schema design procedure on the following reports.

(a)

| Item | RRP ($) | Price ($) | Discount ($) |
|------|---------|-----------|--------------|
| Men's Pants | 59.95 | 40.95 | 19.00 |
| Ladies' Trousers | 59.95 | 55.95 | 4.00 |
| Men's Shirts | 45.50 | 40.95 | 4.55 |
| Socks | 3.50 | 3.50 | |
| Ties | 25.95 | 21.95 | 4.00 |

RRP—Recommended Retail Price

(b)

| Country | Area (sq. km) | Electric power production (Gwhr) | |
|---------|---------------|-----------------|-------|
| | | Hydroelectric | Total |
| Algeria | 2 381 741 | 500 | 4 704 |
| Australia | 7 682 300 | 13 714 | 88 524 |
| Barbados | 430 | - | 264 |
| Brazil | 8 511 965 | 92 943 | 112 572 |

Although not identified by the data supplied it is possible for countries to have the same value in each of the Area, Hydroelectric and Total columns

constraint on 'is child of' would mean that the parent of Ay must be recorded before the first fact can be accepted into the database. So the fact Yuya is the parent of Ay would have to be entered. The mandatory constraint would then mean that the parent of Yuya must be entered before the two facts could become part of the database. As the parent of Yuya is not known then no facts can be accepted by the database. In this case the real life situation that everybody has a parent cannot be enforced as a mandatory constraint as the circular nature of the fact means no data could be stored

(c)

| Location | Code | Fish types | Latitude (°) | Longitude (°) |
|---|---|---|---|---|
| Round Patch | RPTCH | squire snapper amberjack | 27.10221 | 153.32967 |
| Point Lookout Wide | PLWIDE | pearl perch snapper marlin | 27.27828 | 153.41188 |
| Square Patch | SQPTCH | amberjack snapper pearl perch | 27.15091 | 153.36004 |

(d)

### Membership

| Member | Number | Current until |
|---|---|---|
| Green H. | 12323 | 30/6/98 |
| Brown J. | 12324 | 31/1/98 |
| Grey J. | 12325 | 30/6/98 |
| White T. | 12326 | 30/6/98 |
| Black A. | 12327 | |

A. Black is a life member of the club

### Teams

| Team | Manager | Day | Members |
|---|---|---|---|
| A Grade | Grey J. | Monday | Green H. White T. |
| | | Tuesday | Grey J. White T. |
| B Grade | White T. | Wednesday | Brown J. Black A. |

(e)

| Player | Games | Tries | Goals | Field goals | Points |
|---|---|---|---|---|---|
| Steve Renouf | 13 | 15 | | | 60 |
| Laurie Daley | 23 | 11 | 2 | | 48 |
| Mitch Healey | 23 | 7 | 13 | 2 | 56 |
| Jamie Goddard | 10 | 7 | | | 28 |
| Adrian Vowles | 20 | 3 | 2 | | 16 |
| Jamie Ainscough | 25 | 17 | 1 | 2 | 72 |
| Darren Tracey | 23 | 7 | | | 28 |

(f)

| Line | Subject | Class | Teacher | Room |
|------|---------|-------|---------|------|
| 1 | ENG | A | WAL | 24 |
|   | ENG | B | RYA | 18 |
| 2 | MAT | A | GER | 34 |
|   | MAT | B | STO | 35 |
| 3 | IPT |   | GLY | 37 |
|   | JAP |   | SCH | 39 |
|   | GER |   | RYA | 24 |

Three letter codes are used to represent subjects and teachers. Class labelling is only required when two or more classes of the same subject exist on the same line of the timetable

# Reference schemes

Now that uniqueness and mandatory constraints have been discussed it is worthwhile revisiting the topic of reference schemes. A reference scheme shows the relationship between values and entities. It has also been stated that if the reference scheme provides a unique value for each entity then that reference scheme can be the primary reference scheme and can be shown in brackets after the entity type name on the schema diagrams. Reference schemes, though, have further constraints placed upon them. To illustrate these constraints consider the following report from a universe of discourse involving a secondary school.

| Student no. | Surname | First name | Form |
|-------------|---------|------------|------|
| 94001 | Black | Alison | 11A |
| 94002 | Brown | Mary | 11B |
| 94003 | Brown | Brian | 11B |
| 94005 | Brown | Ellen | 11C |
| 94006 | Brown | John | 11B |
| 94007 | Gold | Mary | 11A |

This report would be represented by the following diagram:

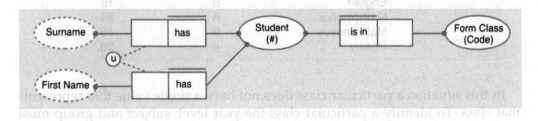

This schema without the primary reference schemes shown in brackets would be:

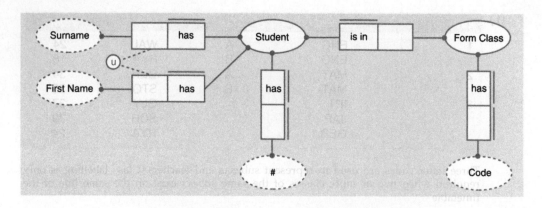

As illustrated in the above diagram, a primary reference scheme will always have a **mandatory** one-to-one relationship with the entity type. If two schemes provide this type of relationship then one must be selected as the primary reference scheme. In the previous example there are two mandatory one-to-one reference schemes for the Student entity type, Student number (#) and the combination of Surname and First Name. The Student number is said to be a simple reference scheme—it requires only one value. The combination of Surname and First Name is referred to as a compound reference scheme as it is made up of more than one value. The Student number should be selected as the primary reference scheme because it is simpler (i.e. contains less values). Simple reference schemes reduce the complexity of a database, making it easier to implement.

In some situations no simple reference scheme exists. Consider, for example, the following Class location report:

| Year | Subject | Group | Room |
| --- | --- | --- | --- |
| 12 | English | A | 12 |
| | English | B | 15 |
| | Mathematics | A | 45 |
| | Mathematics | B | 35 |
| | Geography | A | 12 |
| 11 | English | A | 12 |
| | English | B | 15 |
| | Mathematics | A | 35 |
| | Mathematics | B | 45 |
| | History | A | 28 |

In this situation a particular class does not have a single value that represents that class. To identify a particular class the year level, subject and group must be specified. Therefore, the Class entity type would have a compound reference scheme that consists of these three values. The elementary fact for this report would be:

Class with Year 12 for Subject 'English' and Group 'A' meets in Room (#) 12 or as stated before, in this text, the reference schemes can be specified first.

## Reference schemes
Class (Year, Subject, Group), Room (#)

## Fact
Class 12, 'English', 'A' meets in Room 12

This elementary fact would result in the following schema:

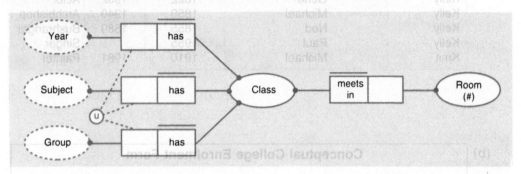

Always having to specify three values can be cumbersome and time-consuming. Another way of dealing with entity types with compound reference schemes is to create a value that provides a simple primary reference scheme. For example, an arbitrary number could be assigned to each class as a unique identifier. But more sensibly a code that embodies the information held in the compound reference scheme could be created. In the previous case the first class could be referred to as '12EngA'. The first two characters give the Year, the next three characters represent the Subject and the last character shows the Group. Introducing this coding system would produce the following elementary facts:

Class (Code) '12EngA' has Year (#) 12
Class (Code) '12EngA' has Subject (Name) 'English'
Class (Code) '12EngA' has Group (Code) 'A'
Class (Code) '12EngA' meets in Room (#) 12

These elementary facts would produce the following schema:

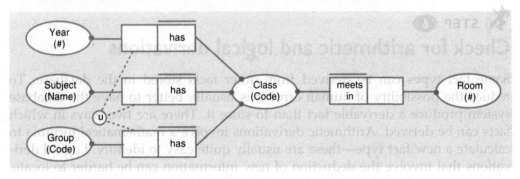

## EXERCISE 14

### Question 1

Perform the first five steps of the conceptual schema design procedure on the following reports.

(a)

| Surname | First name | Born | Died | Occupation |
|---------|-----------|------|------|-----------|
| Kellerman | Annette | 1886 | 1975 | Swimmer |
| Kelly | Gene | 1822 | 1982 | Actor |
| Kelly | Michael | 1850 | 1940 | Archbishop |
| Kelly | Ned | 1855 | 1880 | Bushranger |
| Kelly | Paul | 1955 | | Singer |
| Kmit | Michael | 1910 | 1981 | Painter |

(b)

**Conceptual College Enrolment Form**

Student's surname: _____ Given name(s): _____

Date of birth: _____ Country of birth: _____

Address   Street: _____

          Suburb: _____

          Postcode: _____

Telephones Home: _____

          Guardian's work: _____

Religion: _____

Starting year: _____ Entry year level: _____

As no data is supplied, assumptions will have to be made regarding the necessity of recording certain facts in this database

 STEP 6

# Check for arithmetic and logical derivations

Some fact types can be derived from other facts stored in the database. To reduce the possibility of human error it is usually better to have the database system produce a derivable fact than to store it. There are two ways in which facts can be derived. Arithmetic derivations involve a mathematical formula to calculate a new fact type—these are usually quite easy to identify. Logical derivations that involve the deduction of new information can be harder to locate.

# Arithmetic derivations

Consider the following situation concerning the pricing structure in a retail store.

| Item | RRP ($) | Price ($) | Discount ($) |
|---|---|---|---|
| Blue Jeans | 59.95 | 40.95 | 19.00 |
| Embroidered Shirts | 32.95 | 20.00 | 12.95 |
| Character Ties | 12.95 | 11.95 | 1.00 |
| Cartoon Socks | 4.50 | 3.50 | 1.00 |

RRP—Recommended Retail Price

This data would produce the following schema:

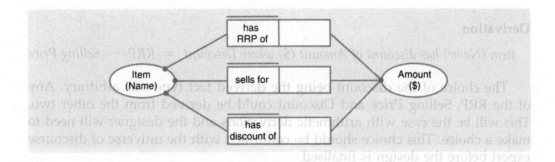

The discount, though, can be calculated from the recommended retail price and the selling price using the formula *Discount = RRP − Price*. Therefore, rather than storing the discount the system can calculate it when required. There are two alternative representations to show derivations. The first representation involves the placing of an asterix (*) beside the derived role and writing the rule used to calculate it on the schema, as shown in the following figure.

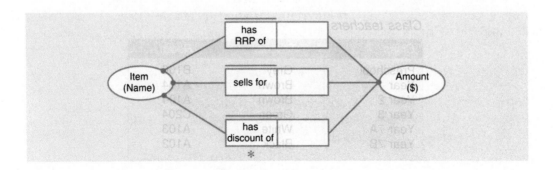

**Derivation**

*Discount = RRP − Sale Price*

Here it is easy to match the rule with the derived role by the use of similar words in the rule and the role. The alternative representation removes the derived fact type from the schema. As the role does not appear on the schema the entities concerned with the derivation rule must be identified as part of the rule, as shown in the following figure.

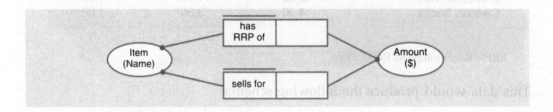

**Derivation**

*Item (Name) has discount of Amount ($) where Discount = RRP − Selling Price*

The choice of the discount being the derived fact type was arbitrary. Any of the RRP, Selling Price and Discount could be derived from the other two. This will be the case with arithmetic derivations and the designer will need to make a choice. This choice should be confirmed with the universe of discourse expert before the design is finalised.

# Logical derivations

Logical derivations can exist when fact types form a loop containing three or more entity types, as in the following universe of discourse which includes Class–Teacher allocation and room utilisation in a primary school.

*Class teachers*

| Class | Teacher | Room |
|-------|---------|------|
| Preschool | Grey | B106 |
| Year 1 | Brown | A104 |
| Year 2 | Brown | A104 |
| Year 3 | Green | C204 |
| Year 7A | White | A103 |
| Year 7B | Black | A102 |

**Room utilisation**

| Room | Teacher |
|------|---------|
| Hall | |
| A101 | Magenta |
| A102 | Black |
| A103 | White |
| A104 | Brown |
| B106 | Grey |
| C204 | Green |

The reports would produce the following schema:

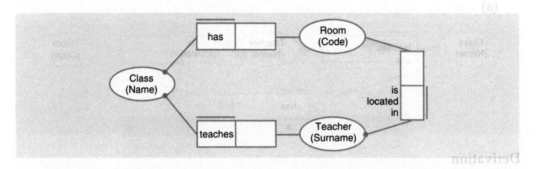

It would seem reasonable that we could derive one of the fact types from this situation. Logical derivations are not like the arithmetic derivations in which the choice is arbitrary. Consider first trying to derive the fact type on the right of the above diagram, the 'Teacher is located in Room'. The derivation rule could be:

Teacher is located in Room
   if a Teacher teaches a Class
   and *that* Class has a Room

This would appear to work for most teachers but what of Magenta? This teacher does not teach a class but is located in a room. This room–teacher relationship would not be able to be deduced using the rule, therefore the 'Teacher is located in Room' is not able to be derived from the other two facts. Examining the situation carefully shows that the lack of a mandatory role constraint on 'teaches' and 'has' (class) prevents this derivation.

Now let us consider trying to derive the 'Class has Room' fact type. The rule could be:

Class has Room
   if a Teacher teaches a Class
   and that Teacher is located in a Room

This rule will work for all situations given in the sample data. This fact type can be derived. The key to locating logical derivations is the placement of the uniqueness and mandatory role constraints.

*A logical derivation of a fact type can be made if it joins the beginning and the end of a chain of roles that each have a mandatory role constraint and a uniqueness constraint on the first role (that is, ⊙▭ ).* The following diagram redraws the schema for the previous example, making the chain of roles more obvious.

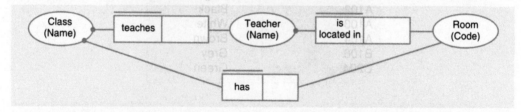

The derivation for the previous example could be shown in either of two ways:

(a)

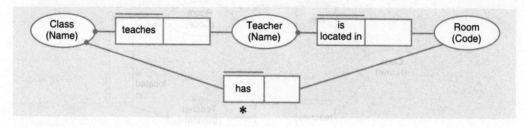

### Derivation

Class has Room
 if a Teacher teaches a Class
 and that Teacher is located in a Room

(b)

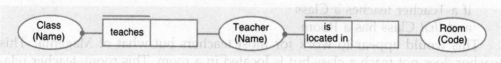

### Derivation

Class has Room
 if a Teacher teaches a Class
 and that Teacher is located in a Room

## EXERCISE 15

### Question 1

Perform the first six steps of the conceptual schema design procedure on the following reports.

(a)

| Year | City | Budget ($) | Total ($) |
|------|------|-----------|-----------|
| 1998 | Brisbane | 120 000 | |
| | Canberra | 100 000 | |
| | Sydney | 220 000 | 440 000 |
| 1999 | Brisbane | 180 000 | |
| | Canberra | 120 000 | |
| | Sydney | 120 000 | 420 000 |

(b)

| Item | Wholesale ($) | Markup ($) | Retail ($) |
|------|--------------|-----------|-----------|
| 1/0 sinkers | 1.25 | 0.50 | 1.75 |
| 2/0 sinkers | 1.25 | 0.50 | 1.75 |
| 6/0 hooks | 2.35 | 0.65 | 2.95 |
| 4/0 hooks | 2.25 | 0.65 | 2.85 |

(c)

| City | Department |
|------|-----------|
| Brisbane | Production |
| Sydney | Promotions |
| Canberra | Administration |
| Canberra | Accounts |
| Melbourne | Assembly |
| Hobart | Packaging |

| Employee | Department | City |
|----------|-----------|------|
| T. Green | Administration | Canberra |
| K. Black | Production | Brisbane |
| D. Grey | Production | Brisbane |
| T. Black | Packaging | Hobart |

(d)

| Tile | Length (cm) | Breadth (cm) | Area (sq. cm) | Tiles per sq. metre |
|------|-------------|--------------|---------------|---------------------|
| Floor | 20 | 20 | 400 | 25 |
| Wall | 25 | 20 | 500 | 20 |
| Frieze | 20 | 5 | 100 | 100 |
| Cork | 20 | 20 | 400 | 25 |

(e)

| Player | Games | Tries | Goals | Field goals | Points |
|---|---|---|---|---|---|
| Steve Renouf | 13 | 15 | | | 60 |
| Laurie Daley | 23 | 11 | 2 | | 48 |
| Mitch Healey | 23 | 7 | 13 | 2 | 56 |
| Jamie Goddard | 10 | 7 | | | 28 |
| Adrian Vowles | 20 | 3 | 2 | | 16 |
| Jamie Ainscough | 25 | 17 | 1 | 2 | 72 |
| Darren Tracey | 23 | 7 | | | 28 |

 STEP **7**

# Add other constraints

There are a number of other constraints that can be added at this time. Value, Frequency, Subset, Equality, Exclusion and Subtype constraints will be considered. Further constraints are possible but are extremely rare and/or overly complex to be considered here.

## Value constraints

A **value** constraint is a listing of the allowed values for an entity type. For example, the entity type Gender could be restricted to the values F and M representing the entities female and male respectively. This would be shown on a schema as a list of the values enclosed in parentheses, as shown in the following figure.

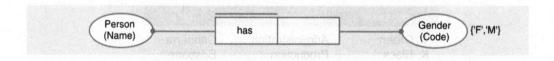

In essence, value constraints could exist for all entity types, but only those that are easily specified are entered on the schema. In the previous example, it may be possible to specify all the acceptable names for the entity type Person but would serve no useful purpose when schematising the universe of discourse.

Where the values being specified form a *subrange* of some existing data type, then they can be expressed by stating the first and last value with two dots between, showing continuance. For example, the days of the working week could be expressed as {'Monday' .. 'Friday'}, allowable ratings could be {'A' .. 'E'} and years could be defined using {0 .. 2000}.

# Frequency constraints

**Frequency** constraints define the number of times a particular role can be played. For example, in a particular school it is a requirement that each senior student must study six subjects. This can be shown on a schema by placing the digit 6 beside the role 'studies' as shown in the next diagram:

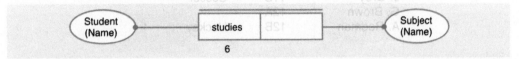

Subranges of integers can be used to specify the minimum and maximum number of times a role can be played. For example, in another school senior students must study at least five subjects but may have up to seven subjects—this would be shown as follows.

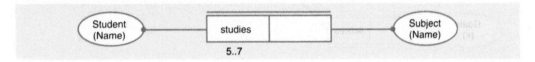

Where the minimum number of times a role can be played is one, the frequency constraint can be specified by using the less than (<) or less than or equal to (≤) mathematical symbols. For example, if a school catered for part-time students, and the only restriction on the number of subjects studied was that they do not exceed seven, the frequency constraint would be shown as follows.

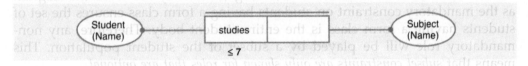

# Subset constraints

A **subset** constraint shows that a particular role can only be played by an entity if another role is also played by that entity. The following report shows information about students and the sport they play. One fact stored about students is the number of goals they have scored. The recording of this fact is dependent on the student playing the sport (i.e. you cannot score goals if you aren't playing a sport). Notice also though that not all students who play sport have scored goals. Therefore, there exists a subset constraint between the roles 'plays' and 'scores'. This is to say that the set of students that score goals is a subset of the set of students that play a sport. The subset constraint is shown on the schema as a dotted line from the role that can be played to the role that must be played with an arrow pointing to the prerequisite role, as shown in the following schema.

*Sport report*

| Student | Form class | Sport | Goals |
|---------|-----------|-------|-------|
| T. Green | 11C | Hockey | 3 |
| R. White | 11A | | |
| S. White | 11C | Soccer | 1 |
| H. Black | 11C | Hockey | - |
| J. Grey | 11B | Soccer | - |
| G. Brown | 12A | | |
| A. Redman | 12B | Hockey | 1 |

Schema produced:

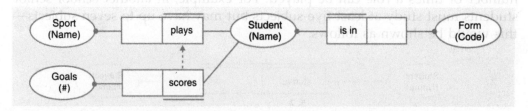

In this case the uniqueness constraint on the role 'scores' has been drawn under the role. This was done so that the constraints are separate and easier to read. This should be done wherever possible to increase the clarity of the schema.

There are other subset constraints that exist in this situation. It would be correct to say that the set of students doing sport is a subset of the students that have a form class. This constraint, though, is already shown on the diagram as the mandatory constraint on students having a form class ensures the set of students having a form class is the entire student body. Therefore, any non-mandatory role will be played by a subset of the student population. This means that *subset constraints are only shown for roles that are optional*.

## Equality constraints

An **equality** constraint shows that a particular role will also be played by an entity if it plays another role. Consider the following report showing information about playground duty done by teachers in a particular primary school.

| Teacher | Room | Class | Duty |
|---------|------|-------|------|
| L. Grey | 101 | | |
| K. Brown | 103 | Year 1 | Monday lunch |
| M. White | 105 | Year 2 | Tuesday morning tea |
| T. Black | 104 | Year 3 | Monday lunch |
| P. Brown | 106 | Year 4 | Friday lunch |

In this school only the class teachers perform playground duty and all class teachers are given a duty. This constitutes an equality constraint between 'teaches' role and the 'does' (playground duty) role. The equality constraint is shown as a double-headed dotted arrow joining the roles involved with the equality constraint. This is shown in the following schema representing the previous report.

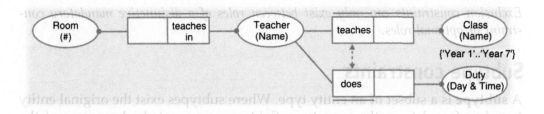

This diagram shows that someone who is a class teacher must do playground duty and that conversely anyone who does playground duty is a class teacher. As was the case for subset constraints, *equality constraints are only shown between optional roles.*

# Exclusion constraints

An **exclusion** constraint prohibits an entity from playing a role if it plays another and vice versa. Consider the following report that shows student allocations for the non-academic Wednesday afternoon session in a senior school.

*Wednesday afternoon student enrolments*

| Student | Form class | Sport | Activity |
|---------|-----------|-------|----------|
| T. Green | 11C | Netball | |
| R. White | 11A | | Philately |
| S. White | 11C | Netball | |
| H. Black | 11C | Swimming | |
| J. Grey | 11B | | Philately |
| G. Brown | 12A | | Chess |
| A. Redman | 12B | Netball | |

Here a student may do a sport or an activity, but not both. Therefore, there exists an exclusion constraint between the 'plays' (sport) role and the 'does' (activity) role. The exclusion constraint is shown as a dotted line between the roles with a circled X in the middle, as shown in the following diagram.

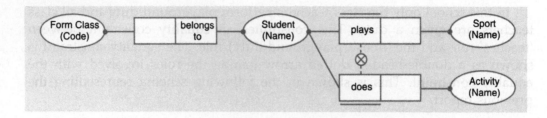

*Exclusion constraints can only exist between roles of a disjunctive mandatory constraint or optional roles.*

## Subtype constraints

A **subtype** is a subset of an entity type. Where subtypes exist the original entity type is referred to as the **supertype**. Subtypes are created when some of the entities have facts to be stored about them that differ from the rest of the entities in that entity type. Subtypes are usually used to qualify an optional role. Consider the following report from a primary school.

| Staff | Position | Room | Extension | Class | Duty |
|---|---|---|---|---|---|
| L. Grey | Principal | 101 | 245 | | |
| T. Smith | Deputy | 101 | 246 | | |
| G. Harrow | Secretary | 102 | 234 | | |
| K. Brown | Teacher | 103 | | Year 1 | Monday lunch |
| M. White | Teacher | 105 | | Year 2 | Tuesday morning tea |
| T. Black | Teacher | 104 | | Year 3 | Monday lunch |
| P. Brown | Teacher | 106 | | Year 4 | Friday lunch |

This could be represented with the following schema:

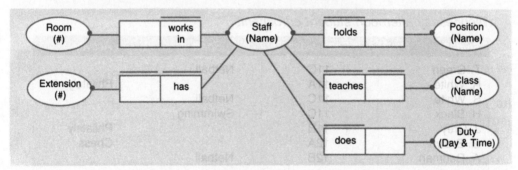

This diagram fails to show that Class and Duty are only stored for teachers and that the extensions are only recorded for non-teaching or administrative staff. Subtyping allows this distinction to be made on the schema. In this case there are two subtypes of the supertype Staff. They could be labelled Teaching and Administrative staff and would be shown as follows.

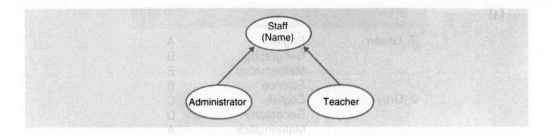

These subtypes must be defined in terms of at least one role played by the super-type. Here the role 'holds' allows the definition of the subtypes as:

each Administrator is a Staff who holds Position 'Principal', 'Deputy' or 'Secretary'

each Teacher is a Staff who holds Position 'Teacher'

The completed schema would be as follows:

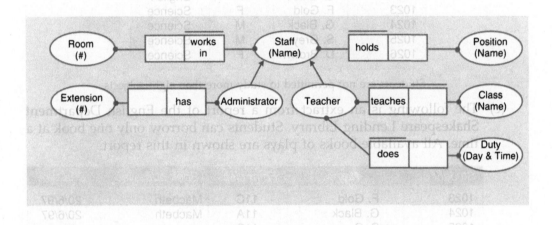

### Subtypes

each **Administrator** is a Staff who holds Position 'Principal', 'Deputy' or 'Secretary'

each **Teacher** is a Staff who holds Position 'Teacher'

## EXERCISE 16

### Question 1

Perform the first seven steps of the conceptual schema design procedure on the following reports.

(a)

| Student | Subject | Grade |
|---------|---------|-------|
| T. Green | English | A |
| | Geography | B |
| | Mathematics | E |
| | Science | B |
| J. Grey | English | C |
| | Geography | D |
| | Mathematics | A |
| | Science | A |

Grades: A—excellent, B—very good, C—good, D—poor, E—very poor

(b)

| Student no. | Name | Gender | Subject |
|-------------|------|--------|---------|
| 1023 | F. Gold | F | English |
| 1024 | G. Black | M | English |
| 1025 | S. Grey | M | English |
| 1026 | D. Brown | F | English |
| 1027 | G. Black | F | English |
| 1023 | F. Gold | F | Science |
| 1024 | G. Black | M | Science |
| 1025 | S. Grey | M | Science |
| 1026 | D. Brown | F | Science |

Students are not permitted to study more than eight subjects

(c) The following is an extract from a report of the English Department Shakespeare Lending Library. Students can borrow only one book at a time. All available books of plays are shown in this report.

| Student no. | Name | Form class | Book borrowed | Due date |
|-------------|------|------------|---------------|----------|
| 1023 | F. Gold | 11C | Macbeth | 20/6/97 |
| 1024 | G. Black | 11A | Macbeth | 20/6/97 |
| 1025 | S. Grey | 11C | | |
| 1026 | D. Brown | 10D | Hamlet | 23/5/97 |
| 1027 | D. White | 10D | | |
| 1028 | G. Silver | 11A | King Lear | 6/6/97 |
| 1029 | H. Green | 10A | | |
| 1030 | G. Lavender | 12A | Richard the Third | 20/6/97 |

(d)

| Student no. | Name | Form class | Adult entry | Guardian | Attendance | Car registration |
|---|---|---|---|---|---|---|
| 1023 | F. Gold | 11C | Y | | F/T | OAS234 |
| 1024 | G. Black | 11A | N | Mr & Mrs N. Black | | |
| 1025 | S. Grey | 11C | N | Mrs J. Brown | | |
| 1026 | D. Brown | 10D | N | Mrs J. Brown | | |
| 1027 | D. White | 10D | Y | | P/T | |
| 1028 | G. Silver | 11A | Y | | F/T | 365ALL |
| 1029 | H. Green | 10A | Y | | P/T | 879CAR |
| 1030 | G. Lavender | 12A | N | Mr & Mrs R. Lavender | | |

F/T—full-time
P/T—part-time

(e) Questions (b), (c) and (d) are all concerned with different aspects of the one school. If one database is to be designed for the whole school the three reports must be considered together. Draw a conceptual schema that includes all three reports.

(f)

| Employee no. | Name | Gender | Driver's licence no. | Parking space |
|---|---|---|---|---|
| 673 | T. Johns | M | 1234126 | |
| 674 | G. Adams | F | 4532435 | 2 |
| 675 | H. Graham | M | | |
| 676 | M. James | M | 2565434 | 3 |
| 677 | D. Alan | F | 2334345 | |
| 678 | M. Francis | F | 3249867 | |
| 679 | L. Barry | M | | 1 |

Ten parking spaces are available numbered 1 to 10

(g) *Athletic records*

| Event | Age | Athlete | Distance (metres) | Time (sec) |
|---|---|---|---|---|
| 100 Metres | 13 | Q. Green | | 12.3 |
| | 14 | A. Brown | | 12.2 |
| 200 Metres | 13 | H. Gold | | 25.1 |
| | 14 | A. Brown | | 25.1 |
| Javelin | 13 | F. Black | 10.3 | |
| | 14 | K. Grey | 11.4 | |
| Shot Put | 13 | Q. Green | 4.6 | |
| | 14 | W. White | 4.8 | |

# STEP 8

# Perform final checks

Final checks of the schema are made in this step of the conceptual schema design procedure. The schema is checked to ensure it is internally consistent, externally consistent, free of redundancy and complete. The schema is **internally consistent** if the constraints do not contradict one another. Consider the following schema which is not internally consistent.

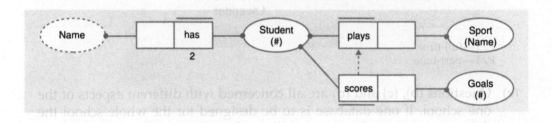

Here the subset constraint is contradicted by the mandatory role constraints (i.e. if both roles are played by all students, then every student must have the number of goals scored stored—it may be zero). Therefore, a subset constraint cannot exist on the 'scores' role. Also the frequency constraint on 'has' contradicts the uniqueness constraint that has also been placed on this role. Either the student has two names stored or only one name.

The second check is for external consistency. The schema is said to be **externally consistent** if it agrees with the original information supplied to design the database. The schema should be systematically checked using the supplied information. This can include population checks not already performed and checking the strength of constraints against the data.

The schema is then checked to ensure it is free of redundancy. The schema is free of redundancy if no elementary fact can appear twice. This can involve checking for repeated entities—so far undetected arithmetic and logical derivations.

Finally, the schema is checked for completeness. The schema is said to be complete if it fulfils all the original requirements of the database. This can be checked by going through each requirement and identifying an element or elements of the schema that satisfy this requirement. If this is done for all requirements then the schema will be complete.

This step is a check and if all the preceding seven steps have been done correctly then it will produce no change to the schema. There is a temptation to skip this step presuming that all the other steps have been done correctly but for any problem solving exercise it is good practice to stand back and take another look at the problem and your solution at the end of the process.

## EXERCISE 17

### Question 1

Perform the conceptual schema design procedure on the following reports.

(a) *Employee earnings*

| Employee no. | Name | Type | Hourly rate ($) | Hours | Level | Weekly pay ($) |
|---|---|---|---|---|---|---|
| 001 | T. Mackay | Salary | | | AD03 | 546.80 |
| 002 | H. Cairns | Wage | 13.67 | 40 | | 546.80 |
| 003 | T. Hobart | Wage | 12.78 | 35 | | 447.30 |
| 004 | G. Darwin | Salary | | | AD04 | 689.00 |
| 005 | D. Adelaide | Salary | | | AD03 | 592.60 |
| 006 | A. Sydney | Wage | 13.67 | 40 | | 546.80 |
| 007 | L. Brisbane | Wage | 12.78 | 40 | | 511.20 |

There exist five administrative officers award levels AD01 to AD05

*Company cars*

| Car no. | Make | Model | Registration no. | Employee |
|---|---|---|---|---|
| 1 | Mitsubishi | Magna | 387 DAJ | 001 |
| 2 | Mitsubishi | Pajero | 963 DGH | 002 |
| 3 | Nissan | Patrol | 783 DES | 006 |
| 4 | Mitsubishi | Magna | 672 DGY | 007 |

All cars belonging to the company are shown in this table

(b)

| Atomic no. | Element | Form | Hardness | Molecular formula | Melting point (°C) | Boiling point (°C) |
|---|---|---|---|---|---|---|
| 2 | Helium | Gas | - | He | - | −269 |
| 3 | Lithium | Metal | 0.6 | | 179 | 1340 |
| 4 | Beryllium | Metal | 7 | | 1285 | 2970 |
| 5 | Boron | Crystal | 9 | | 2370 | - |
| 8 | Carbon | Crystal | 10 | | 3730 | 4840 |
| | | Solid | 1 | | 3600 | - |
| 7 | Nitrogen | Gas | - | $N_2$ | −210 | −196 |
| 8 | Oxygen | Gas | - | $O_2$ | −218 | −182 |
| 9 | Fluorine | Gas | - | $F_2$ | −223 | −188 |

(c)

| Number | Name | Date | Treatment | Employee |
|---|---|---|---|---|
| 001 | J. Green | 30/6/97 | Cut | Jessie |
| 002 | J. Gold | 30/6/97 | Tint | Marie |
| 003 | N. Black | 30/6/97 | Style | Jessie |
| 002 | J. Gold | 7/7/97 | Style | Jessie |
| 004 | N. White | 8/7/97 | Cut | Marie |

(d)

| Registration | Year | Description | Used | Odometer | Price ($) |
|---|---|---|---|---|---|
| 234 ASC | 1996 | Nissan Pulsar Sedan | Y | 24 234 | 15 954 |
| 832 DQA | 1997 | Nissan Pulsar Sedan | | | 19 995 |
| 245 BER | 1995 | Mitsubishi Pajero | Y | 86 123 | 29 990 |
| 536 DYT | 1996 | Nissan Patrol | | | 45 998 |
| 348 AST | 1997 | KIA Sportage | Y | 24 234 | 24 678 |

(e)

**Account no:** 18276326
**Name:** ADDAMS Marie Louise
**Address:**   35 Gomez St
          Lurchville

| Date | Transaction | Credit ($) | Debt ($) | Current balance ($) |
|---|---|---|---|---|
| 29/6/97 | Balance | | | 84.85 |
| 30/6/97 | Deposit | 123.95 | | 208.80 |
| 30/6/97 | Withdrawal | | 50.00 | 158.80 |
| 1/7/97 | Cheque (12343) | | 34.85 | 123.95 |
| 7/7/97 | Deposit | 123.95 | | 197.90 |
| 8/7/97 | Withdrawal | | 50.00 | 73.95 |

(f)   A small school library runs on a card system that consists of three components.

Accession Register—contains one card for each book. The accession number is unique for each book in the library (i.e. there could be a number of copies of *Macbeth* but each copy would have a different accession number).

Shakespeare, William          104.2 SHA

  *Macbeth*

**Cost:** $12.50          **Accession No:** 12675

Book Label—allows the recording of the borrower (identified by name and form class).

| Shakespeare, William | | 104.2 SHA |
|---|---|---|
| *Macbeth*<br>12675 | | |
| **Name** | **Form** | **Due date** |
| ~~N. Green~~ | ~~11A~~ | ~~12/8/97~~ |
| R. Black | 11A | 26/8/97 |

Form List—books borrowed are recorded against the student's name.

| Form: 11A | |
|---|---|
| **Student** | **Books** |
| D. Adams | 45642 |
| R. Black | 12675, 23233 |
| T. Brown | |
| N. Green | ~~12675~~ |

The conceptual schema created using the conceptual schema design procedure gives a complete representation of the universe of discourse for a particular system. Systems are emerging that will allow the direct implementation of conceptual schema into database systems, but unfortunately those systems are not yet easily available or widely distributed. Therefore, to implement a conceptual schema it must first be mapped into a logical schema. One such logical schema is the relational schema, derived from the relational model of data.

## The relational model

In the relational model all data is stored in named tables, which are also called relations. Each table consists of unnamed horizontal rows and named vertical columns. The data in the tables is arranged so that it has one (and only one)

# CHAPTER 3

# Relational implementation

Take me to your base.

The conceptual schema created using the conceptual schema design procedure gives a complete representation of the universe of discourse for a particular system. Systems are emerging that will allow the direct implementation of conceptual schema into database systems, but unfortunately these systems are not yet easily available or widely distributed. Therefore, to implement a conceptual schema it must first be mapped into a logical schema. One such logical schema is the relational schema, derived from the relational model of data.

## The relational model

In the relational model all data is stored in named tables, which are also called relations. Each table consists of unnamed horizontal rows and named vertical columns. The data in the tables is arranged so that it has one (and only one) value at each intersection of a row and a column, called a cell. Each row in a table must be unique. A **key** is a column, or combination of columns, that uniquely defines each row of a table. That is, the data contained in the key is not repeated in another row of the table. The following example shows two tables.

**Students**

| Name | Level | Class | Position |
|------|-------|-------|----------|
| A. Green | 12 | A | Captain |
| B. Brown | 12 | B | Prefect |
| C. Black | 11 | A | |
| D. Grey | 12 | B | |
| E. Gold | 11 | A | |

**Subjects**

| Student | Subject |
|---------|---------|
| A. Green | English |
| A. Green | Mathematics |
| A. Green | Science |
| B. Brown | English |
| B. Brown | Mathematics |
| B. Brown | Geography |

The Students table has five rows and four columns whereas the Subjects table has six rows and two columns. The key for the Students table is the column Name (i.e. there would only be one row per student in this table and names would not be repeated). A key consisting of one column is referred to as a simple key. The Subjects table has a key that is made up of two columns, Student and Subject, because a combination of the values in these columns is needed to uniquely define a row. Keys consisting of more than one column are called compound keys. If in a table you have more than one column or combination of columns that uniquely define a row, then a primary key must be chosen. If the keys differ in length (number of columns involved) then the simplest (fewest number of columns) key should be chosen as the primary key. Where keys are of the same length then one must be selected using other criteria.

A **relational schema** is a set of table definitions that describes all tables for a particular database. The table definitions consist of the table name followed by a list of the column names enclosed in round brackets. The above tables would be defined as follows:

Students (Name, Year Level, Class, Position)
Subjects (Student, Subject)

A relational schema also shows the constraints on the data. The system used, in this text, is closely related to the system used to represent constraints on conceptual schema. The *uniqueness constraint* is shown as a bar (optionally arrowed) placed under the *key*. Following is an example:

Students (<u>Name</u>, Year Level, Class, Position)
Subjects (<u>Student, Subject</u>)

*Mandatory constraints* are indicated by writing OP underneath any optional columns. Any columns without this annotation are mandatory. A simple key by definition cannot be optional and will not have OP beneath it. However, it is possible (though rare and not desirable) to have optional columns in a compound key. An example of this follows:

Students (<u>Name</u>, Year Level, Class, Position)

OP

Subjects (<u>Student, Subject</u>)

*Value constraints* are shown by writing the constraint above the column to which it applies. *Frequency constraints* are shown by defining them at the bottom of the relational schema. An example of this follows:

{1..12}    {'A','B','C'}

Students (<u>Name</u>, Year Level, Class, Position)

OP

Subjects (<u>Student, Subject</u>)

## Constraints

A student can study no more than six subjects

Other constraints such as *subset, equality, exclusion, external uniqueness* and *disjunctive mandatory* constraints are shown using the dotted line notation joining the columns concerned. The following shows a relational schema showing some of these types of constraints.

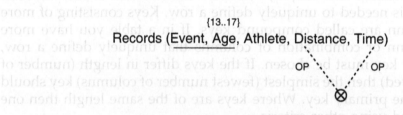

{13..17}

Records (<u>Event, Age, Athlete</u>, Distance, Time)

OP            OP

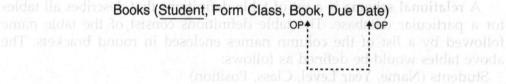

Books (<u>Student, Form Class, Book</u>, Due Date)

OP            OP

The first example shows an exclusion constraint and the second an equality constraint.

A column (or combination of columns) from one table whose values form the primary key in another table is referred to as a **foreign key**. Foreign keys should be shown on relational schema using the subset constraint arrow. Returning to the earlier example, the student name is the primary key of the Students table and these names appear in the Student column of the Subjects table. This would be shown as follows:

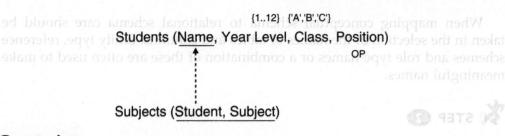

Students (<u>Name</u>, Year Level, Class, Position)

Subjects (<u>Student, Subject</u>)

## Constraints

A student can study no more than six subjects

The foreign key constraint will ensure the student exists in the Students table before subjects can be added to the Subjects table for that student.

# The relational mapping procedure

The **Relational Mapping Procedure** (RMAP) is also known as the **Optimal Normal Form** (ONF) **algorithm**. This is a simple procedure that guarantees redundancy-free relational design. It consists of three steps.
- Step 1—Compound uniqueness constraints
- Step 2—Simple uniqueness constraints
- Step 3—Constraints

 **STEP ①**

# Compound uniqueness constraints

All fact types with compound uniqueness constraints are placed in separate tables. The primary key of each table is based on the compound uniqueness constraint. To keep track of which role types have already been mapped a line is drawn around the roles for each table. For example, consider the following schema for the situation considered earlier.

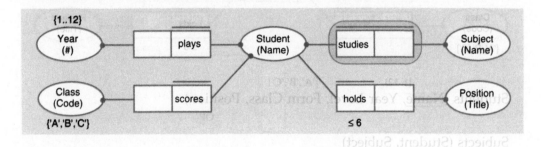

Step 1 would produce the following table definition.
Subjects (<u>Student, Subject</u>)

When mapping conceptual schema to relational schema care should be taken in the selection of the names of tables and columns. Entity type, reference schemes and role type names or a combination of these are often used to make meaningful names.

 STEP ❷

# Simple uniqueness constraints

Fact types with simple uniqueness constraints attached to the same entity type, including nested entity types, are grouped into the same table. The key for each of these tables is based on the central entity type. Step 2 for the previous example would produce:

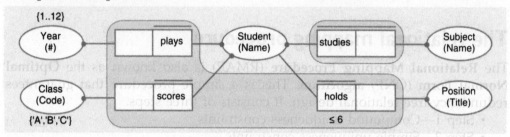

Student (<u>Name</u>, Year Level, Class, Position)

 STEP ❸

# Constraints

Finally, the constraints and derivations marked on the conceptual schema are mapped onto the relational schema. The previous example would become:

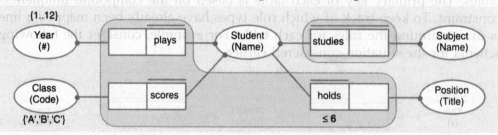

Students (<u>Name</u>, Year Level, Form Class, Position)

OP

Subjects (<u>Student, Subject</u>)

## Constraints
A student can study no more than six subjects

# Nested fact types

Nested fact types initially appear to be covered by Steps 1 and 2 (i.e. they have a compound uniqueness constraint and can involve simple fact types as in the following diagram).

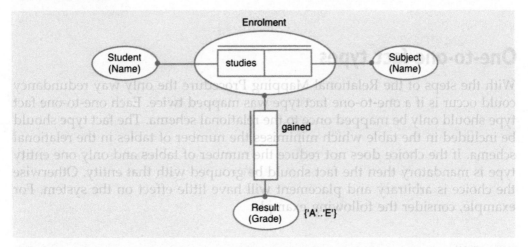

Nested fact types themselves are not considered as part of Step 1. The compound uniqueness constraint forms a nested object type. The compound uniqueness constraint becomes important when specifying the keys for the tables formed. As in the case of compound uniqueness constraints in Step 1, all entity types involved in the constraint are used in the key. The previous example would use Step 2 of the Relational Mapping Procedure and have the following relational schema.

{'A'..'E'}

Results (<u>Student</u>, <u>Subject</u>, Result)

If the nested object type plays a many-to-many relationship with another object type then Step 1 of the process will apply, for example:

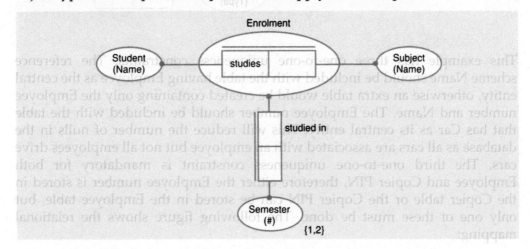

Here Step 1 would produce

{1,2}

Enrolments (<u>Student, Subject, Semester</u>)

# One-to-one fact types

With the steps of the Relational Mapping Procedure the only way redundancy could occur is if a one-to-one fact type was mapped twice. Each one-to-one fact type should only be mapped once to the relational schema. The fact type should be included in the table which minimises the number of tables in the relational schema. If the choice does not reduce the number of tables and only one entity type is mandatory then the fact should be grouped with that entity. Otherwise the choice is arbitrary and placement will have little effect on the system. For example, consider the following example:

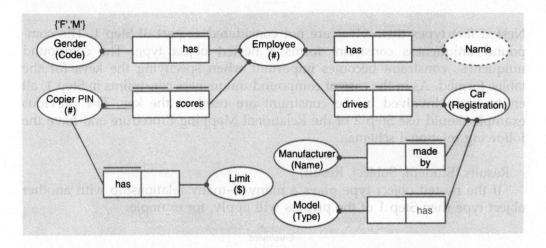

This example has three one-to-one uniqueness constraints. The reference scheme Name should be included with the table having Employee as the central entity, otherwise an extra table would be created containing only the Employee number and Name. The Employee number should be included with the table that has Car as its central entity. This will reduce the number of nulls in the database as all cars are associated with an employee but not all employees drive cars. The third one-to-one uniqueness constraint is mandatory for both Employee and Copier PIN, therefore either the Employee number is stored in the Copier table or the Copier PIN can be stored in the Employee table, but only one of these must be done. The following figure shows the relational mapping:

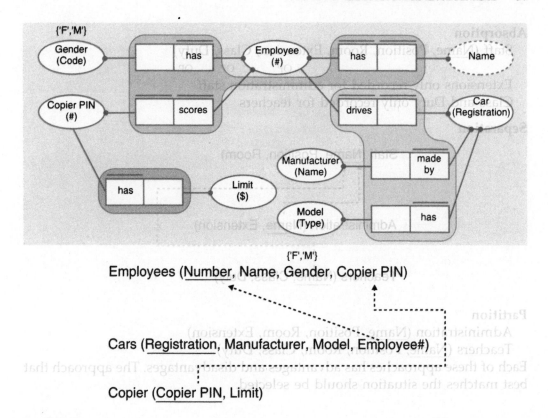

{'F','M'}
Employees (<u>Number</u>, Name, Gender, Copier PIN)

Cars (<u>Registration</u>, Manufacturer, Model, Employee#)

Copier (<u>Copier PIN</u>, Limit)

# Subtypes

Subtypes can be handled in three ways by using *absorption, separation* or *partition*. Absorption is the collapsing of the subtypes back into the supertype and rules written to define when columns can have optional values. Separation is where the subtypes are treated as entity types and tables based on the subtypes are created. Partition can be used when the subtypes are exclusive (have no entities in common) and exhaustive (all the entities in the supertype are contained in subtypes). With partition, a table which contains all the information is created for each subtype. The following example, which has been considered before, shows how each method would be applied to a particular situation.

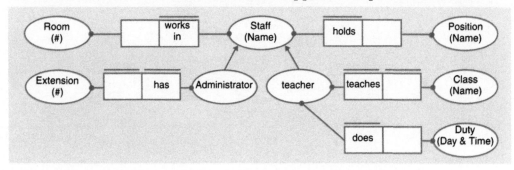

### Absorption
Staff (<u>Name</u>, Position, Room, Extension, Class, Duty)

                                         OP        OP     OP

Extensions only recorded for administration staff
Class and Duty only recorded for teachers

### Separation

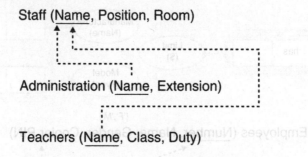

Staff (<u>Name</u>, Position, Room)

Administration (<u>Name</u>, Extension)

Teachers (<u>Name</u>, Class, Duty)

### Partition
Administration (<u>Name</u>, Position, Room, Extension)
Teachers (<u>Name</u>, Position, Room, Class, Duty)

Each of these approaches has advantages and disadvantages. The approach that best matches the situation should be selected.

### EXERCISE 18

### Question 1
Obtain a relational schema from the following conceptual schema by applying the steps of the Relational Mapping Procedure.

(a)

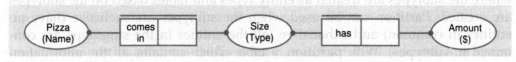

(b)

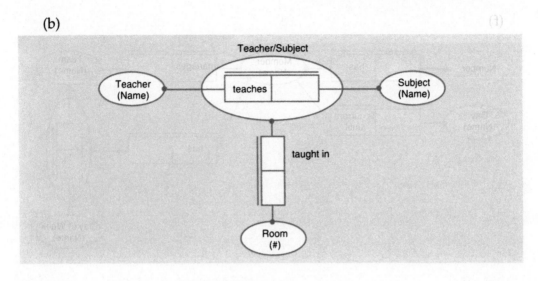

(c)

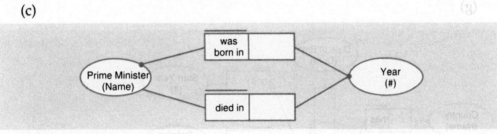

(d)

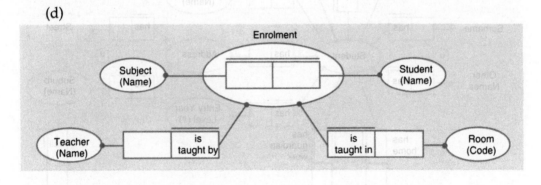

(e)

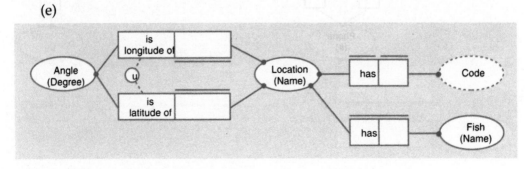

**(f)**

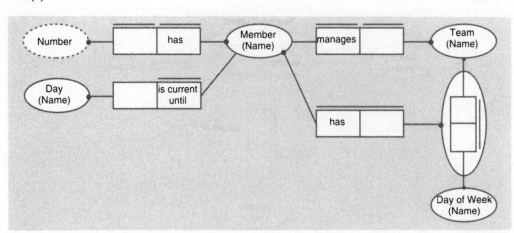

**(g)**

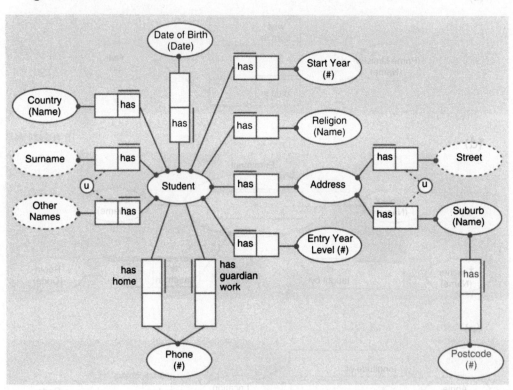

(h)

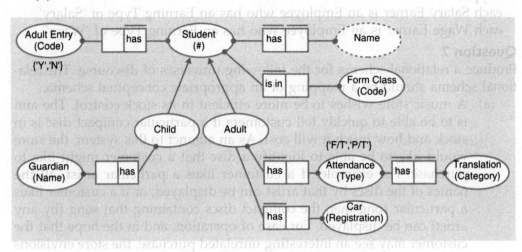

## Subtypes

each Child is a Student who has an Adult Entry code of 'N'
each Adult is a Student who has an Adult Entry code of 'Y'

(i)

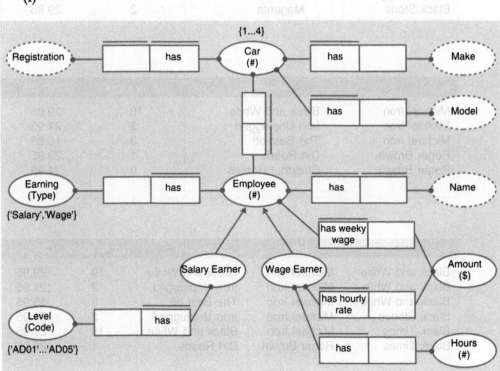

## Subtypes

each Salary Earner is an Employee who has an Earning Type of 'Salary'
each Wage Earner is an Employee who has an Earning Type of 'Wage'

## Question 2

Produce a relational schema for the following universes of discourse. The relational schema should be a mapping of an appropriate conceptual schema.

(a) A music store wishes to be more efficient in its stock control. The aim is to be able to quickly tell customers if a particular compact disc is in stock and how much it will cost. As an adjunct to this system, the store would like to be able to identify a disc that a customer might like to purchase. For example, if a customer likes a particular artist, all the names of the discs by that artist can be displayed, or if a customer likes a particular song then the compact discs containing that song (by any artist) can be displayed. For ease of operation, and in the hope that the customer may see an interesting unrelated purchase, the store envisions the display as scrolling alphabetical lists as shown in the following reports.

| Album | Artist | No. in stock | Cost ($) |
|---|---|---|---|
| Black and White | Michael Iron | 10 | 29.95 |
| Black or Blue | Gina Greentrees | 0 | 15.95 |
| Iron Unplugged | Michael Iron | 2 | 21.95 |
| Black Stone | Magenta | 2 | 29.95 |
| : | : | : | : |

| Artist | Album | No. in stock | Cost ($) |
|---|---|---|---|
| Michael Iron | Black and White | 10 | 29.95 |
| Michael Iron | Iron Unplugged | 2 | 21.95 |
| Michael Iron | The Best of! | 3 | 15.95 |
| Roger Brown | Dirt Roads | 1 | 29.95 |
| Roger Brown | Chestnut Horses | 0 | 24.95 |
| : | : | : | : |

| Song | Artist | Album | No. in stock | Cost ($) |
|---|---|---|---|---|
| Black and White | Michael Iron | Black and White | 10 | 29.95 |
| Black and White | Michael Iron | Iron Unplugged | 2 | 21.95 |
| Black and White | Michael Iron | The Best of! | 3 | 15.95 |
| Black Stones | Michael Iron | Iron Unplugged | 2 | 21.95 |
| Black Times | Michael Iron | Black and White | 10 | 29.95 |
| Black Times | Roger Brown | Dirt Roads | 1 | 29.95 |
| : | : | : | : | : |

(b) A technical college wants to computerise its information on courses, students and staff. Following are some of the reports expected to be available on the system. Each has a small sample population, but this should not be considered significant (i.e. some assumptions will have to be made).

## Courses

| Subject | Name | Contact | Credit | Year | Semester | Lecturer |
|---------|------|---------|--------|------|----------|----------|
| IT100 | Info Systems 1 | 2 lectures 1 tutorial | 10 | 1997 | 1 | Thompson |
| IT101 | Programming 1 | 3 lectures 1 tutorial | 12 | 1997 | 2 | Green |
| IT200 | Info Systems 2 | 3 lectures | 10 | 1997 | 1 | Thompson |
| : | : | : | : | : | : | : |

**Note:** each subject is only offered in one semester

## 1997 timetable

| Semester | Subject | Type | Room | Time |
|----------|---------|------|------|------|
| 1 | IT100 | L | 23 | Mon. 10 am Thurs. 12 midday |
| | IT100 | T | 100 | Wed. 4 pm Tues. 3 pm Thurs. 4 pm |
| 2 | IT101 | L | 23 | Tues. 10 am Tues. 11 am Fri. 10 am |
| | IT101 | T | 100 | Thurs. 11 am |

Type L—lecture, T—tutorial; each is of one hour duration

## Students

| Number | Surname | First name | Course | Date of birth | Subjects | Year | Result |
|--------|---------|------------|--------|---------------|----------|------|--------|
| 47346 | Green | Judy | Dip. IT | 12.10.79 | IT100 | 1996 | 6 |
| | | | | | IT101 | 1996 | 5 |
| | | | | | IT131 | 1996 | 1 |
| | | | | | IT200 | 1997 | 0 |
| | | | | | IT201 | 1997 | 0 |
| | | | | | IT131 | 1997 | 0 |
| 76467 | Brown | Gary | Cert IT | 4.6.80 | IT100 | 1997 | 0 |
| | | | | | IT115 | 1997 | 0 |

Results on a 1 to 7 scale with 0 being recorded when results are not available

**Lecturers**

| Surname | First name | Title | Department | Phone |
|---------|-----------|-------|------------|-------|
| Green | Robyn | Dr | Computer Science | 2376 |
| Thompson | Thomas | Mr | Communication | 1956 |
| Brown | Bronwyn | Ms | Computer Science | 4398 |

(c) The following reports describe the universe of discourse for a milk vendor who delivers to households.

**Prices**

| Product | Size | Price (cents per unit) |
|---------|------|------------------------|
| Full cream | 600 mL | 80 |
| | 1 litre | 123 |
| | 2 litre | 241 |
| Trim | 600 mL | 84 |
| | 1 litre | 129 |
| | 2 litre | 255 |
| Skim | 600 mL | 84 |
| | 1 litre | 131 |
| | 2 litre | 259 |
| 100% Orange juice | 2 litre | 420 |
| 25% Orange juice | 2 litre | 225 |

**Orders**

| Street | Number | Name | Day | Product | Size | Quantity |
|--------|--------|------|-----|---------|------|----------|
| White | 2 | G. Smith | Mon. | Trim | 1 litre | 1 |
| | | | Wed. | Trim | 1 litre | 1 |
| | | | Fri. | Trim | 1 litre | 2 |
| | 4 | A. Grey | Mon. | Skim | 2 litre | 2 |
| | | | Wed. | Trim | 1 litre | 1 |
| | | | Fri. | Skim | 2 litre | 1 |
| | | | | Full cream | 1 litre | 1 |
| Gregory | 2 | G. Smith | Tues. | Full cream | 600 mL | 2 |
| | | | Thurs. | Full cream | 600 mL | 2 |
| | | | Sat. | Full cream | 600 mL | 2 |

No deliveries on Sunday

## Customer accounts

| Customer name: A. Grey |
| --- |
| Address: 4 White Street |
| Week ending: 21.6.97 |

| Product | Size | Price (¢) | Quantity | Cost |
| --- | --- | --- | --- | --- |
| Full cream | 600 mL | 80 | | |
| | 1 litre | 123 | 1 | $1.23 |
| | 2 litre | 241 | | |
| Trim | 600 mL | 84 | | |
| | 1 litre | 129 | 1 | $1.29 |
| | 2 litre | 255 | | |
| Skim | 600 mL | 84 | | |
| | 1 litre | 131 | | |
| | 2 litre | 259 | 3 | $7.77 |
| 100% Orange juice | 2 litre | 420 | | |
| 25% Orange juice | 2 litre | 225 | | |
| | | | Amount due: | $10.29 |

### (d) Gas account

| | Customer number: 3948743 |
| --- | --- |
| | Amount due: $83.35 |
| | Date due: 28/1/97 |

**Customer details**

Ms G. Green
4 White Street
Rainbowville

**Details of Invoice**
Date of issue: 10/1/97  Invoice no: 83645  Reading date: 8/1/97  Next reading: 8/4/97

**Location**   4 White Street, Rainbowville

| Meter readings: | Present | Previous | Used | MJ factor | MJs used |
| --- | --- | --- | --- | --- | --- |
| | 1725 | 1605 | 120 | 39.36 | 4 723 |
| Charges | | | | | |
| First | 1 824 MJs @ 2.308¢ per MJ | | 42.10 | | |
| Next | 1 824 MJs @ 1.532¢ per MJ | | 27.94 | | |
| Remainder | 1 075 MJs @ 1.242¢ per MJ | | 13.35 | | |
| Total due 20/1/97 | | | $83.35 | | |

# Glossary

**arity**  the property of a particular fact that describes the number of roles played

| | | |
|---|---|---|
| unary: | 1 role | e.g. Keith swims |
| binary: | 2 roles | e.g. Maxine exercises by walking |
| ternary: | 3 roles | e.g. Peter has a black belt in karate |
| quaternary: | 4 roles | e.g. Ben practises judo during lesson 4 on Thursday |

**assumptions**  communication device between the database designer and the universe of discourse expert. Assumptions state the database designer's interpretations of a universe of discourse where some aspects are not made clear by the information provided, such as when output reports are not significant. Assumptions must be clearly stated on the schema

**conceptual information processor**  enforces the conceptual schema when changes are made to the system

**conceptual schema**  maps the structure of the universe of discourse by describing it in terms of objects, the roles they play and constraints that affect the objects

**conceptual schema diagram** (CSD)  diagrammatic representation of a conceptual schema, showing objects, roles and constraints

**constraints**  restrict the ways in which data may be stored or altered. The constraints used in this text are:

**disjunctive mandatory roles**  describe an either/or/both situation, to show that an entity must play at least one of the indicated roles. A disjunctive mandatory role may be drawn either by showing lines from the two roles coming together at a dot on the entity type, or through the use of dotted lines linking the roles and meeting at a circled dot

**equality**  indicates that a particular role must be played by an entity if it plays another particular role and vice versa. An equality constraint is indicated by a double-headed dotted arrow

**exclusion**  prohibits an entity from playing a particular role if it plays another particular role and vice versa, that is, only one of the nominated roles can be played. An exclusion constraint is indicated by dotted lines meeting at a circled cross

**frequency**  defines the number of times a role can be played. Frequency constraints are indicated by a fixed number (e.g. 6 indicates that the role must be played exactly 6 times), range (e.g. 5..7 indicates that the role can be played 5, 6 or 7 times), or with $>$, $<$, $\geq$, $\leq$ to indicate minimum or maximum number of times the role is played

**mandatory**  which roles must be played by all entities of an entity type. Mandatory constraints are indicated by a dot placed where the line from the role that must be played by every entity meets the entity type. Nulls in the sample data indicate that care should be taken when assigning mandatory role constraints

**subset**  indicates that a particular role may be played if and only if another particular role is also played by that entity. A subset constraint is indicated by a dotted arrow from the role that may be played to the role that must be played. Subset constraints are only shown where both roles are optional

**subtype**   is a subset of an entity type, known as the supertype. A subtype is usually used to qualify optional roles, when facts are stored for some entities but not others within one entity type

**uniqueness**   restricts to one the number of times an entity can play a particular role. Uniqueness constraints are indicated by bars (which may or may not have arrowheads) drawn over the unique role or combination of roles. Uniqueness constraints are referred to as being either simple (bar spans one role) or compound (bar spans more than one role)

**value**   lists the allowed values for an entity type, and is indicated by curly brackets, for example, {'M','F'} indicates that only values of M (male) and F (female) will be allowed

**database**   a collection of related facts

**derivation rules**   specify information that can be obtained arithmetically or logically from existing data

**derived fact type**   can be obtained from other information stored in the database, for example, calculating the markup from known cost price and selling price

**elementary fact**   a statement that conveys that an object has a property or that one or more objects are related in a particular way. An elementary fact expresses information in its simplest form. An elementary fact cannot be broken into simpler statements without loss of information

**entity**   is an object (tangible or abstract) that forms part of the universe of discourse. Entities are identified using entity type (e.g. Student), reference scheme (e.g. Surname) and value (e.g. Smith)

**entity type**   the set of all instances of an entity

**external consistency**   exists when a conceptual schema agrees with the original information supplied for the universe of discourse

**external schema**   describes how a user views the universe of discourse and its relationship to the conceptual schema. Different users' views of the external schema may be influenced by limitations in their access rights

**foreign key**   a column (or combination of columns) in a table which forms the primary key in another table

**internal consistency**   in a conceptual schema exists when constraints do not contradict one another

**internal schema**   specifies how data are stored and accessed for a particular universe of discourse

**key**   a column (or combination of columns) that uniquely defines each row of a table. The data contained in the key is not repeated in another row of the table

**logical schema**   derived from the conceptual schema and expressing the universe of discourse in a manner which can be implemented using an appropriate model such as a relational model

**nested entity type**   considers a relationship between two entities to be an entity in itself, and hence allows this combination to play one or more roles with other entity types

**Optimal Normal Form algorithm**   a procedure that produces a redundancy-free relational design from a conceptual schema diagram

**redundancy**   occurs when a fact is stored more than once. Data is repeated unnecessarily. Redundancy in an information system can lead to anomalies when data is changed, since it is necessary to update every occurrence of that data. A conceptual schema is free of redundancy when no elementary sentence is represented more than once

**reference scheme** shows the relationship between values and entities in an entity type

**Relational Mapping Procedure** a procedure that produces a redundancy-free relational design from a conceptual schema diagram

**relational schema** a set of table definitions that describes all tables for a particular database

**significant output report** shows data that demonstrates all relationships and constraints for a particular universe of discourse. If an output report is not significant, assumptions may need to be made

**subtype** a subset of an entity type, known as the supertype. A subtype is usually used to qualify optional roles, when facts are stored for some entities but not others within one entity type

**supertype** an entity type in which subtypes can be identified

**transaction** undertaken by issuing an instruction to either add or delete (which may be accepted or rejected if violates constraints) or by posing a question (which will be answered or rejected if it is illegal). Transactions may be either simple (one statement) or compound (a list of statements that are grouped together by placing *begin* and *end* at the start and finish of the list)

**universe of discourse** (UoD) a domain that encompasses all aspects of the information being considered

**universe of discourse expert** someone intimately familiar with the knowledge domain of the universe of discourse and who can be considered an authority for clarification for all aspects of the domain

**value** a character, strings of characters or number which is used to reference entities

# Answers

## EXERCISE

### Question 1

| | | | |
|---|---|---|---|
| (a) | rejected—C1 violated | (n) | Yes |
| (b) | rejected—C3 violated | (o) | No |
| (c) | accepted | (p) | 2 |
| (d) | accepted | (q) | Dooley, Grimes, Rich |
| (e) | accepted | (r) | Yes |
| (f) | accepted | (s) | Hockey |
| (g) | accepted | (t) | Doyle |
| (h) | accepted | (u) | No Sport |
| (i) | accepted | (v) | No Person |
| (j) | accepted | (w) | Yes |
| (k) | rejected—C1 and C4 violated | (x) | Green, Dooley, Alan, Rich, Gibson |
| (l) | Yes | (y) | rejected—C1 violated |
| (m) | Yes | (z) | Brown, Green |

### Question 2

(a) accepted
(b) accepted
(c) accepted
(d) rejected—C2 violated
(e) accepted
(f) Jerry
   Mary
(g) Chris
(h) rejected—C3 violated
(i) Chris
(j) Person X is daughter of Person Y if Y parent of X and X is 'F'
(k) Person X is son of Person Y if Y parent of X and X is 'M'
(l) Person X is grandparent of Person Y if X parent of A and A parent of Y
(m) Person X is grandmother of Person Y if X grandparent of Y and X is 'F'
(n) Person X is grandfather of Person Y if X is grandparent of Y and X is 'M'
(o) Each time you added a person to the database you would have to add their parents, then their parents and then their parents etc. Eventually you would either run out of research on the family tree or perhaps end up at Adam who didn't have parents. Either way you would not be able to supply a parent for a person and the entire update would be rejected by the conceptual information processor.

## EXERCISE 2

**Question 1**

(a)   2

(b)   1

(c)   3

(d)   2

(e)   2 (or could be considered unary)

## EXERCISE 3

**Question 1**

(a) (e) (g) (i) (m)

**Question 2**

Note the choice of words to represent entities, reference modes and roles are not the only possibilities. These answers are provided as a guide to format and content of answers.

(a)   Person (Name) 'Alan G.' was born in Year (Nr) '1975'

(b)   Teacher (Name) 'Gremmin T.' looks after Form (Code) '8A'

(c)   Person (Name) 'Greg' smokes
      Person (Name) 'Alice' is non-smoker

(d)   Car (Model) 'Pajero' is made by Company (Name) 'Mitsubishi'

(e)   Person (Name) 'Green H.' is of Age (Nr) 17
      Person (Name) 'Green H.' belongs to House (Name) 'Henderson'

## EXERCISE 4

**Question 1**

(a)   Person (Name) 'Mandy' has Belief (Status) 'Yes'

(b)   Person (Name) 'Cassy' is of Gender (Type) 'female'

(c)   Person (Name) 'Graham' has Employed (Code) 'Y'

**Question 2**

(a)   Person (Name) 'Gary' has Phone (Nr) 33452321
      Person (Name) 'Gary' lives in Suburb (Name) 'Sunnybank'

(b)   Person (Name) 'David' lives in Suburb (Name) 'Clayfield'
      Suburb (Name) 'Clayfield' is allocated Postcode (Nr) 4011

(c)   Car (Model) 'Pajero' with Cylinders (Nr) 4 can tow Load (Tonne) 1.2

(d)   Language (Name) 'Pascal' was written by Person (Surname) 'Wirth'
      Language (Name) 'Pascal' was written in Year (Nr) 1971

(e)   Author (Name) 'Allen Y.' wrote Book (Title) 'Last Return'
      Book (Title) 'Last Return' costs Price ($) 19.95

(f)   Student (Name) 'Jemma' in Event (Type) '100 M' gained Place (Nr) 1

(g)   Student (Name) 'Jones A.' in Semester (Nr) 1 studied Subject (Name) 'English' gaining a Rating (Grade) 'A'

(h)   Race (Nr) 1 at Track (Name) 'Eagle Farm' was won by Horse (Name) 'Grey Synd'
      Horse (Name) 'Grey Synd' is owned by Person (Name) 'Brown T.'

(i) Book (ISBN) '0 07 470032' is Book (Title) 'New Senior Computer Studies'
Book (ISBN) '0 07 470032' was written by Author (Name) 'Mark Baker'
Book (ISBN) '0 07 470032' has Pages (Nr) 252

(j) Company (Name) 'Software Galore' sells Item (Name) 'Word Maker' in Quantity (Nr) 25

(k) Person (Name) 'John Adam Smith' married Person (Name) 'Mary Elizabeth Jones'
Person (Name) 'John Adam Smith' is parent of Person (Name) 'Wayne John Smith'
Person (Name) 'John Adam Smith' has Gender (Type) 'Male'
(this is only one interpretation—many others are correct)

(l) Horse (Name) 'Anna Dane' has Gender (Type) 'Mare'
Horse (Name) 'Anna Dane' cost Price ($) 100 000

(m) Student (Name) ?????? belongs to House (Name) ??????
Student (Name) ?????? is in Year (Level) 1
Student (Name) ?????? in Event (Name) '50 metre sprint' gained Place (Nr) 1

(n) Student (Name) 'Jones B.' is in Form (Code) '11B'
Form (Code) '11B' meets in Room (Nr) 204
Form (Code) '11B' is supervised by Teacher (Name) 'Glead Y.'

# EXERCISE 5

**Question I**
(d) (e) (f) (g) (h) (i) (j) (l) (m) (n) (o) (p)

**Question 2**
(a) Person (Name) 'Mary Smith' is of Age (Nr) 42

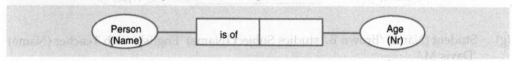

(b) Person (Name) 'Green G.' stands at Height (cm) 170
Person (Name) 'Green G.' weighs Weight (kg) 65

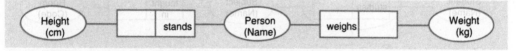

(c) Book (Title) 'Neuromancer' was written by Author (Name) 'W. Gibson'
Book (Title) 'Neuromancer' is of Type (Code) 'Sci-fi'
Book (Title) 'Neuromancer' costs Price ($) 7.95

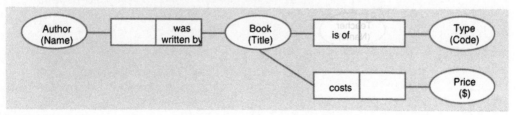

(d)    Pizza (Name) 'Hawaiian' comes in Size (Type) 'Medium'
       Size (Type) 'Medium' costs Price ($) 7.95

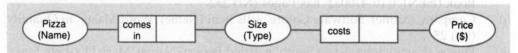

(e)    Student (Name) 'Green A.' in Subject (Name) English received Result (Grade) 'A'

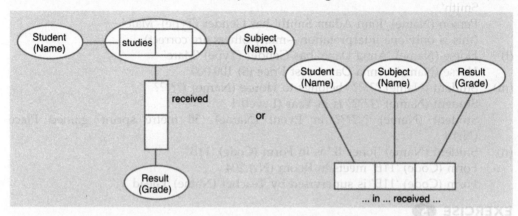

The nested form on the left will be used for the remainder of this text.

(f)    Pizza (Name) 'Hawaiian' requires Topping (Type) 'Ham'

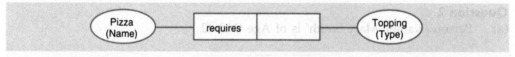

(g)    Student (Name) 'Brown B.' studies Subject (Name) 'English' with Teacher (Name) 'Davis M.'
       Subject (Name) 'English' taught in Room (Code) 'E101'

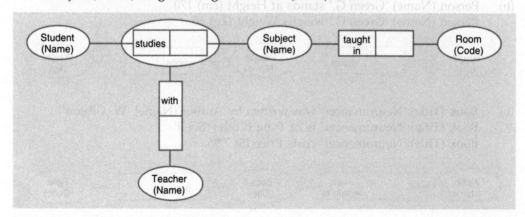

(h)     Year (Level) 12 for Subject (Name) 'English' on Day (Name) 'Monday' meets in
       Lesson (Nr) 1

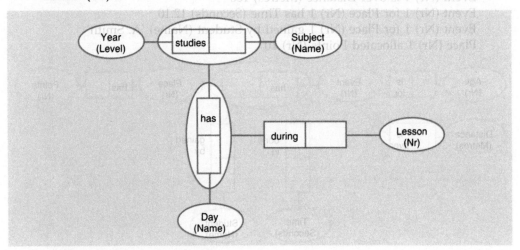

(i)     Customer (Nr) 001 has (Name)
       Video (Nr) 001 has (Title)
       Customer (Nr) 001 borrows Video (Nr) 001 on Day (Date) 1/1/97
       **Note:** designer-supplied data can be used when a verbal description of universe
       of discourse is provided.

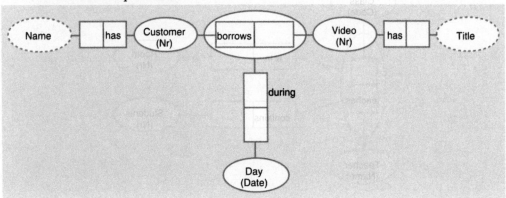

(j)     Item (Name) 'Riders Jeans' has RRP ($) 59.95
       Item (Name) 'Riders Jeans' has Price ($) 40.95
       Item (Name) 'Riders Jeans' has discount ($) 59.95

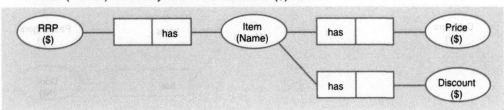

(k)    Event (Nr) 1 is for Age (Nr) 13
       Event (Nr) 1 is over Distance (Metres) 100
       Event (Nr) 1 for Place (Nr) 1 has Time (Seconds) 12.10
       Event (Nr) 1 for Place (Nr) 1 gained by Student (Name) 'A. Smith'
       Place (Nr) 1 allocated Points (Nr) 10

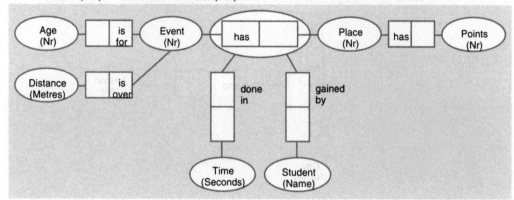

(l)    Teacher (Name) 'Green A.' teaches Class (Code) '11ENG' in Room (Nr)
       Class (Code) '11ENG' taught by Teacher (Name) 'Green A.' contains StuLdents
       (Nr) 25

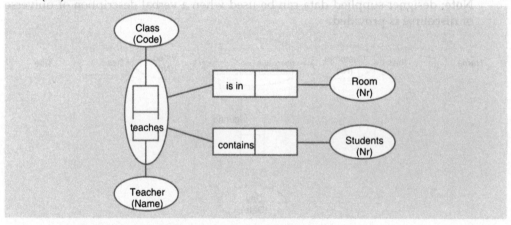

(m)    Car (Model) 'Super Wagon' has Cylinders (Nr) 6
       Car (Model) 'Super Wagon' holds Passengers (Nr) 7
       Car (Model) 'Super Wagon' has Doors (Nr) 5

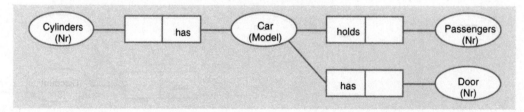

(n)    Lot (Nr) 12 in Street (Name) Barton in Suburb (Name) Clayfield is owned by Person (Name) 'Smyth A.'

Lot (Nr) 12 in Street (Name) Barton in Suburb (Name) Clayfield has size of Area (SqM) 504

**Note:** rearrangement of order to improve readability of fact.

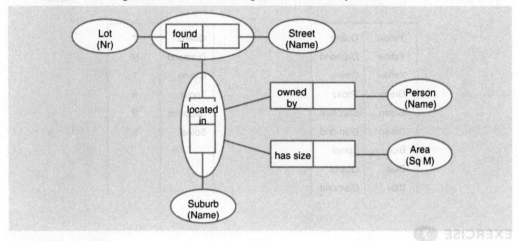

# EXERCISE 6

## Question I

(a)    Artist (Name) 'Celine Dion' recorded Album (Name) 'Falling into You'

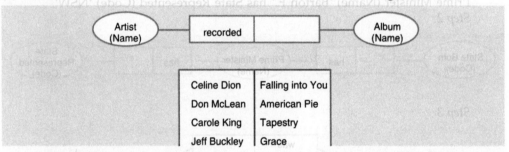

(b)    Movie (Name) 'The Truth about Cats and Dogs' features Actor (Name) 'Uma Thurman'

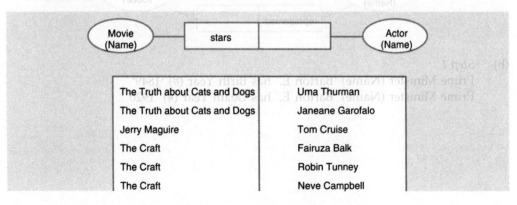

(c)  Stone (Name) 'Quartz' found with Colour (Name) 'Yellow'
     Stone (Name) 'Quartz' is of Hardness (Nr) 7

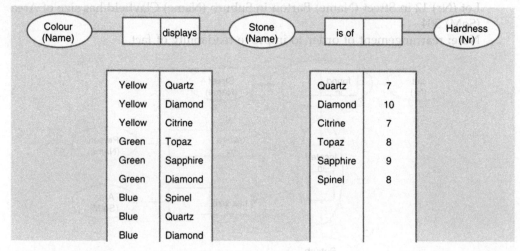

## EXERCISE 7

### Question 1

(a)  *Step 1*
     Prime Minister (Name) 'Barton E.' has State Born (Code) 'NSW'
     Prime Minister (Name) 'Barton E.' has State Represented (Code) 'NSW'
     *Step 2*

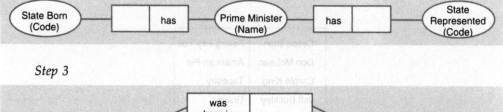

     *Step 3*

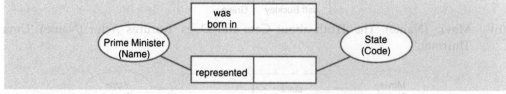

(b)  *Step 1*
     Prime Minister (Name) 'Barton E.' has Birth Year (#) '1849'
     Prime Minister (Name) 'Barton E.' has Death Year (#) '1920'

*Step 2*

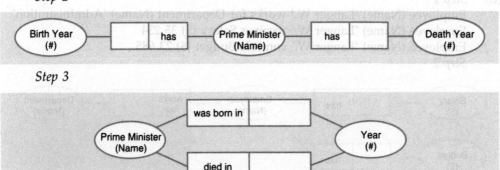

*Step 3*

*(c)* *Step 1*

Manager (Name) 'Brown E.' has Classification (Code) 'PO3'
Manager (Name) 'Brown E.' has Salary ($) 35 271
Manager (Name) 'Brown E.' has Car (Registration) '123 AST'
Manager (Name) 'Brown E.' has Phone Extension (#) 320
Staff (Name) 'Whiting S.' has Classification (Code) 'PO2'
Staff (Name) 'Whiting S.' has Salary ($) 29 235
Staff (Name) 'Flounder A.' has Car (Registration) '134 CAR'
Staff (Name) 'Whiting S.' has Phone Extension (#) 317

*Step 2*

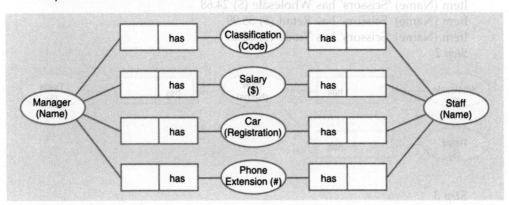

*Step 3*

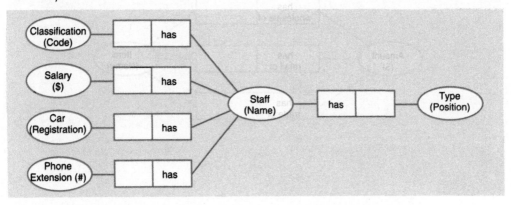

(d)    *Step 1*

Employee (Name) 'Langer W.' works for Department (Name) 'Administration'
Employee (Name) 'Langer W.' receives Salary ($) 35 234
Employee (Name) 'Langer W.' controls Budget ($) 23 685

*Step 2*

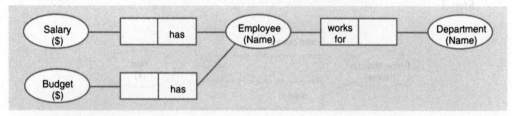

*Step 3*

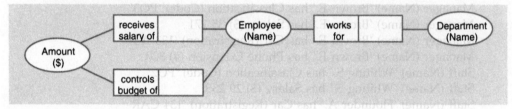

(e)    *Step 1*

Item (Name) 'Scissors' has Wholesale ($) 24.68
Item (Name) 'Scissors' has Retail ($) 35.99
Item (Name) 'Scissors' has Trade ($) 33.69

*Step 2*

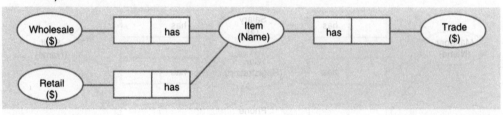

*Step 3*

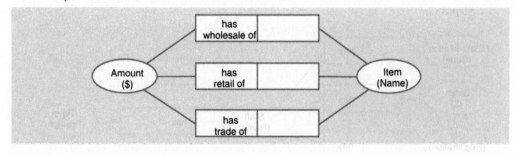

(f)  *Step 1*
Company (Name) 'John's Computers' has Manager (Name) 'John Crook'
Company (Name) 'John's Computers' has Contact (Name) 'John Crook'
Company (Name) 'John's Computers' has Phone (#) 2843 7642
*Step 2*

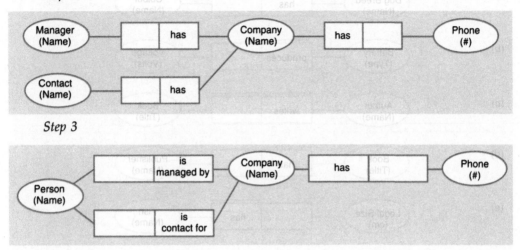

*Step 3*

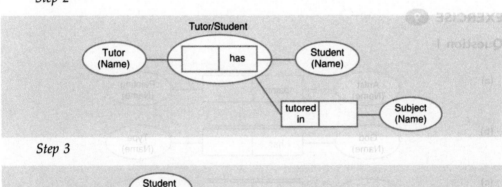

(g)  *Step 1*
Student (Name) 'Addams M.' has Tutor (Name) 'Jones T.' for Subject (Name)
'English'
*Step 2*

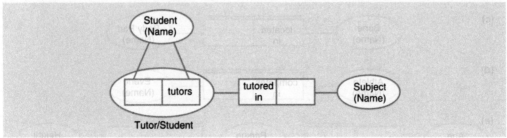

# EXERCISE 8

## Question 1

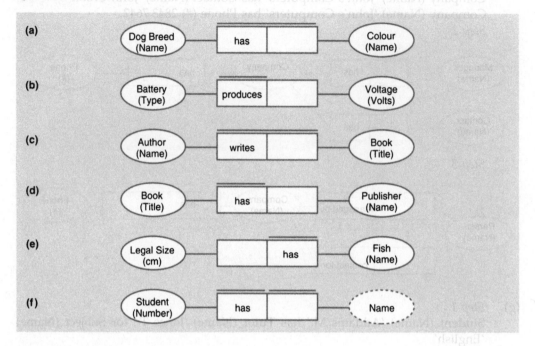

(a) Dog Breed (Name) — has — Colour (Name)

(b) Battery (Type) — produces — Voltage (Volts)

(c) Author (Name) — writes — Book (Title)

(d) Book (Title) — has — Publisher (Name)

(e) Legal Size (cm) — has — Fish (Name)

(f) Student (Number) — has — Name

# EXERCISE 9

## Question 1

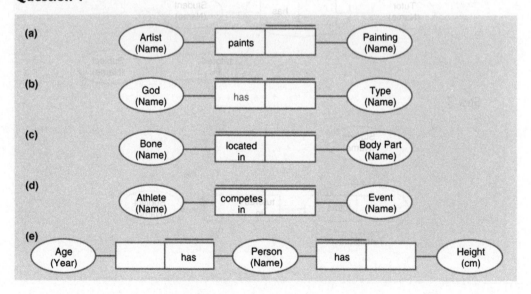

(a) Artist (Name) — paints — Painting (Name)

(b) God (Name) — has — Type (Name)

(c) Bone (Name) — located in — Body Part (Name)

(d) Athlete (Name) — competes in — Event (Name)

(e) Age (Year) — has — Person (Name) — has — Height (cm)

## EXERCISE ⑩

### Question I

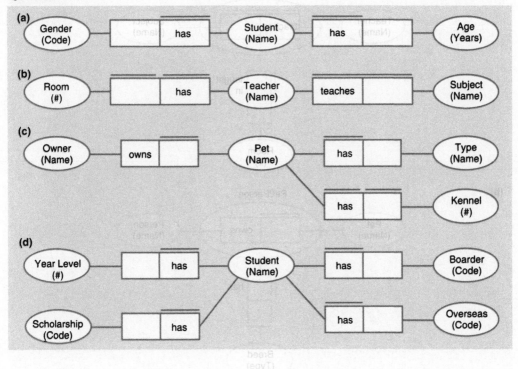

## Question 2

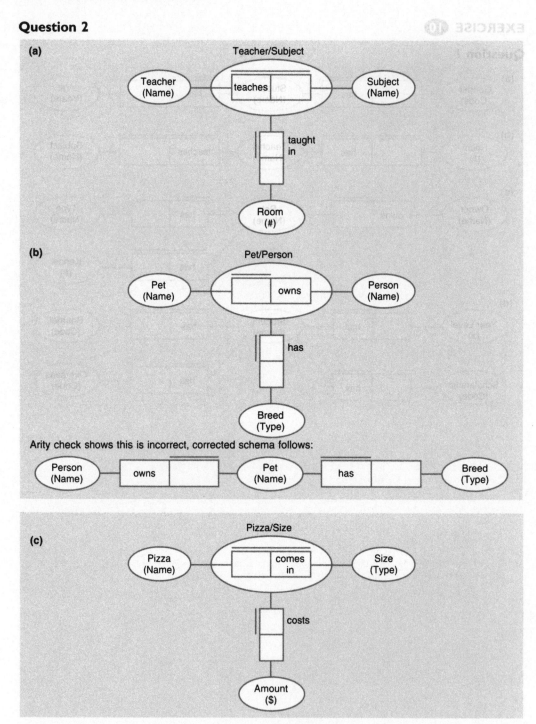

(a) Teacher/Subject

Teacher (Name) — teaches — Subject (Name)

taught in

Room (#)

(b) Pet/Person

Pet (Name) — owns — Person (Name)

has

Breed (Type)

Arity check shows this is incorrect, corrected schema follows:

Person (Name) — owns — Pet (Name) — has — Breed (Type)

(c) Pizza/Size

Pizza (Name) — comes in — Size (Type)

costs

Amount ($)

Arity check does not indicate a problem but examining the table shows that the price is only related to the size of the pizza and not the type; the corrected schema follows.

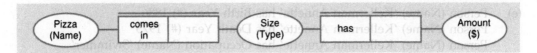

## Question 3

(a)    Prime Minister (Name) 'Barton E.' has State Born (Code) 'NSW'
       Prime Minister (Name) 'Barton E.' has State Represented (Code) 'NSW'

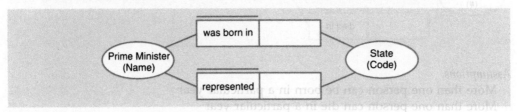

(b)    Prime Minister (Name) 'Barton E.' has Year Born (Code) '1849'
       Prime Minister (Name) 'Barton E.' has Year Died (Code) '1920'

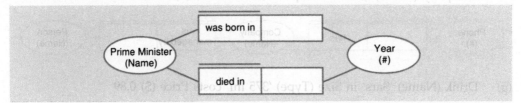

(c)    Student (Name) 'Harrow W.' for Subject (Name) 'English' has Teacher (Name) '
       Watson'
       Student (Name) 'Harrow W.' for Subject (Name) 'English' is in Room (Code) 'A24'

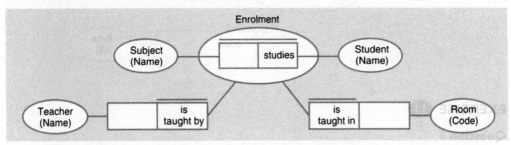

(d)    Employee (Name) 'Langer A.' works for Department (Name) 'Administration'
       Employee (Name) 'Langer A.' receives Salary ($) 35 234
       Employee (Name) 'Langer A.' controls Budget ($) 23 685

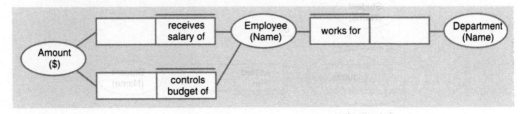

(e)   Person (Name) 'Kellerman Annette' has Birth Year (#) 1886
      Person (Name) 'Kellerman Annette' has Death Year (#) 1975
      Person (Name) 'Kellerman Annette' has Occupation (Name) 'Swimmer'

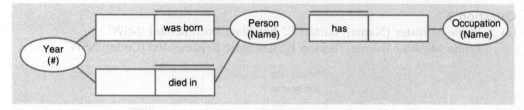

*Assumptions*
   More than one person can be born in a particular year
   More than one person can die in a particular year
   More than one person can have a particular occupation
(f)   Company (Name) 'John's Computers' is managed by Person (Name) 'John Crook'
      Company (Name) 'John's Computers' has Phone (#) 2843 7642

(g)   Drink (Name) 'Sars' in Size (Type) '375 ml' costs Price ($) 0.89

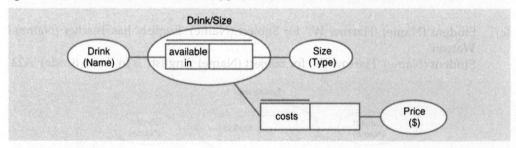

## EXERCISE ⓫

### Question 1
(a)   Student (Name) 'Adams P.' has Tutor (Name) 'Jones T.' for Subject (Name)
      'English'

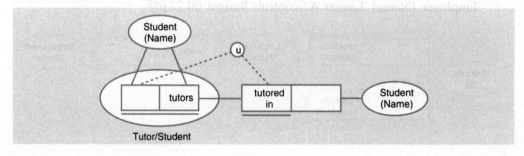

(b)    Student (Name) 'Harold Y.' in Subject (Name) 'English' gained Place (#) 1

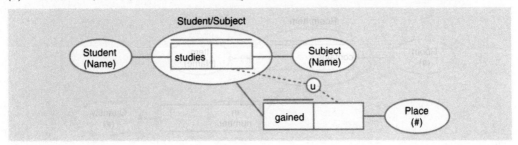

## EXERCISE 12

### Question 1

(a)    Prime Minister (Name) 'Barton E.' was born in Year (#) 1849
       Prime Minister (Name) 'Barton E.' was born in State (Code) 'NSW'

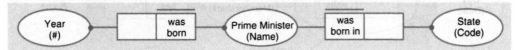

(b)    Student (Name) 'Green T.' in Subject (Name) 'English' for Semester (#) 1 gained
       Result (Grade) 'A'

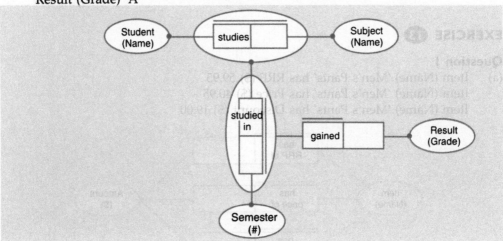

(c)    Prime Minister (Name) 'Forde F.' has Death Age (Year) 93
       Prime Minister (Name) 'Forde F.' was married to Person (Name) 'O'Reilly V.'

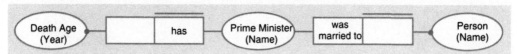

(d)     Room (#) 12 has Item (Name) in Quantity (#) 30

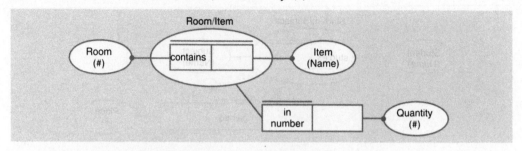

(e)     Person (Membership#) 12845 has (Name) 'Black T.'
        Person (Membership#) 12845 on Day (Date) '12/03/97' paid Amount
        ($) 12.00

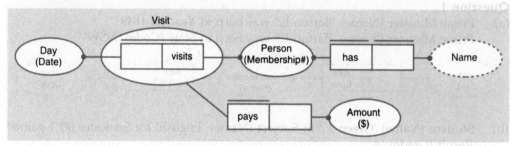

## EXERCISE 13

### Question 1

(a)     Item (Name) 'Men's Pants' has RRP ($) 59.95
        Item (Name) 'Men's Pants' has Price ($) 40.95
        Item (Name) 'Men's Pants' has Discount ($) 19.00

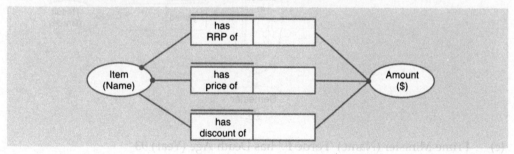

(b)   Country (Name) 'Algeria' has Area (sq. km) 2 381 741
      Country (Name) 'Algeria' produces Hydroelectric Power (Gwhr) 500
      Country (Name) 'Algeria' produces Total Power (Gwhr) 4704

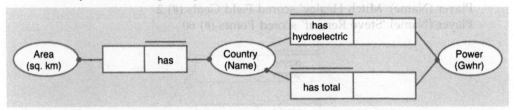

(c)   Location (Name) 'Round Patch' has (Code) 'RPTCH'
      Location (Name) 'Round Patch' has Fish (Name) 'squire'
      Location (Name) 'Round Patch' has Latitude (Degree) 27.10221
      Location (Name) 'Round Patch' has Longitude (Degree) 153.32967

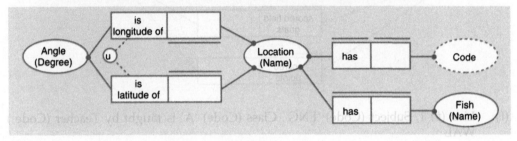

(d)   Member (Name) 'H. Green' has (#) 12323
      Member (Name) 'H. Green' is current until Day (Date) '30/6/98'
      Member (Name) 'J. Grey' manages Team (Name) 'A Grade'
      Team (Name) 'A Grade' on Day of Week (Name) Monday has Member (Name)
      'H. Green'

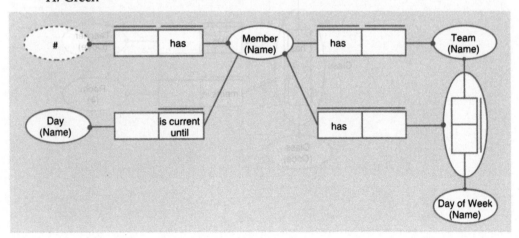

(e)    Player (Name) 'Steve Renouf' played Games (#) 13
       Player (Name) 'Steve Renouf' scored Tries (#) 15
       Player (Name) 'Laurie Daley' scored Goals (#) 2
       Player (Name) 'Mitch Healey' scored Field Goals (#) 2
       Player (Name) 'Steve Renouf' scored Points (#) 60

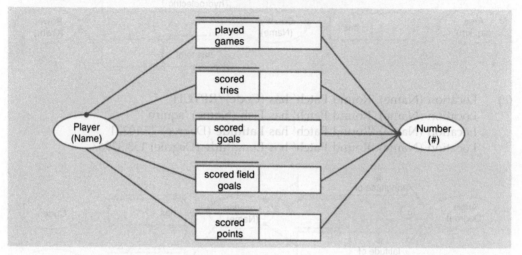

(f)    Line (#) 1, Subject (Code) 'ENG', Class (Code) 'A' is taught by Teacher (Code )
       WAL
       Line (#) 1, Subject (Code) 'ENG', Class (Code) 'A' is conducted in Room (#)

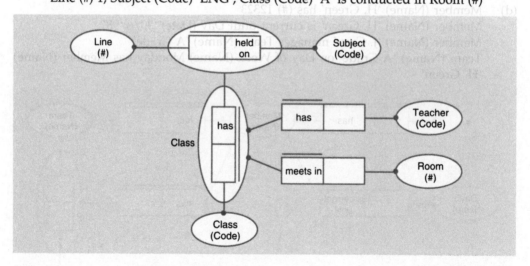

## EXERCISE 14

**Question 1**

(a)  Person with Surname 'Kellerman' and First Name 'Annette' was born in Year (#) 1886

Person with Surname 'Kellerman' and First Name 'Annette' died in Year (#) 1975

Person with Surname 'Kellerman' and First Name 'Annette' works at Occupation (Name) 'Swimmer'

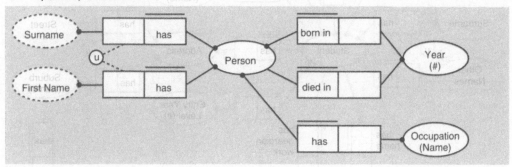

*Assumptions*

More than one person can be born in a particular year

More than one person can die in a particular year

More than one person can have a particular occupation

(b)  *Reference schemes:*

Student (Surname, Given Names), Date of Birth (Date), Country (Name), Address (Street, Suburb), Suburb (Name), Postcode (#), Phone (#), Religion (Name), Year (#), Year Level (#)

*Facts:*

Student 'Green', 'Mary Jane' has Date of Birth 30/6/1964

Student 'Green', 'Mary Jane' was born in Country 'Australia'

Student 'Green', 'Mary Jane' lives at Address '39 Wild Street', 'Clayfield'

Suburb 'Clayfield' has Postcode 4011

Student 'Green', 'Mary Jane' has Home Phone 2343 3624

Student 'Green', 'Mary Jane' has Guardian Work Phone 9843 3493

Student 'Green', 'Mary Jane' has Religion 'Uniting'

Student 'Green', 'Mary Jane' has Start Year 1997

Student 'Green', 'Mary Jane' has Entry Year Level 8

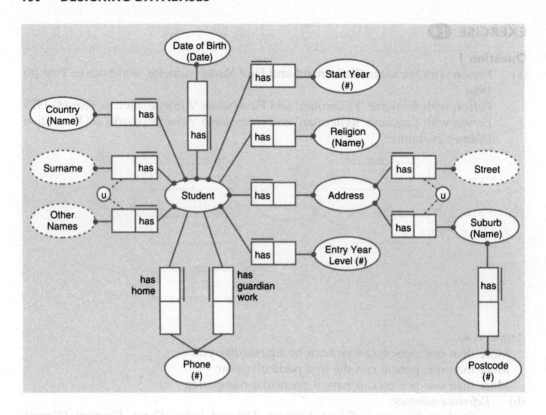

## EXERCISE ⑮

### Question 1

(a) Year (#) 1998 for City (Name) 'Brisbane' has Budget ($) 120 000
Year (#) 1998 has Total Budget ($) 440 000

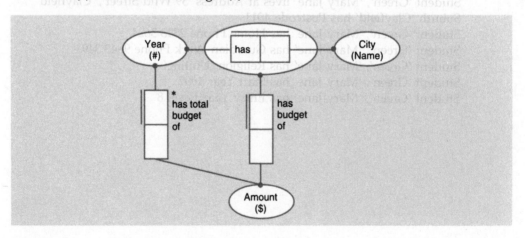

*Assumption*
A total budget can be the same amount for more than one year

*Derivation*
    Total Budget = sum of all city budgets for that year
(b)    Item (Name) '1/0 sinkers' has Wholesale Price ($) 1.25
    Item (Name) '1/0 sinkers' has Markup ($) 0.50
    Item (Name) '1/0 sinkers' has Retail Price ($) 1.75

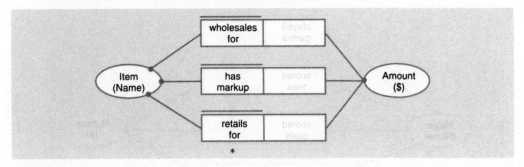

*Derivation*
    Retail Price = Wholesale + Markup
(c)    City (Name) 'Brisbane' is location of Department (Name) 'Production'
    Employee (Name) 'T. Green' works for Department (Name) 'Administration'
    Employee (Name) 'T. Green' works in City (Name) 'Canberra'

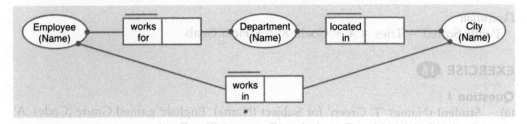

*Derivation*
    An employee works in the city in which his or her Department is located
(d)    Tile (Type) 'Floor' has Length (cm) 20
    Tile (Type) 'Floor' has Breadth (cm) 20
    Tile (Type) 'Floor' has Area (sq. cm) 400
    Tile (Type) 'Floor' has Tiles/sq. metre (#) 25

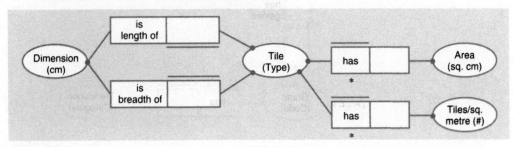

*Derivations*
    Area = Length × Breadth
    Tiles/sq. metre = 10 000 ÷ Area

(e)    Player (Name) 'Steve Renouf' played Games (#) 13
       Player (Name) 'Steve Renouf' scored Tries (#) 15
       Player (Name) 'Laurie Daley' scored Goals (#) 2
       Player (Name) 'Mitch Healey' scored Field Goals (#) 2
       Player (Name) 'Steve Renouf' scored Points (#) 60

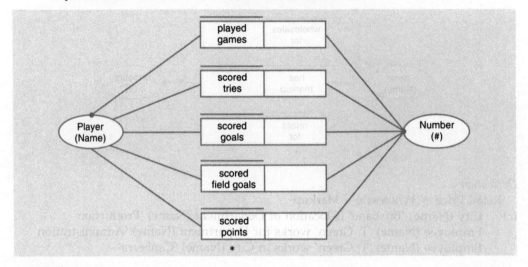

*Derivation*
   Points Scored = Tries × 4 + Goals × 2 + Field Goals

## EXERCISE 16

**Question 1**
(a)    Student (Name) 'T. Green' for Subject (Name) 'English' gained Grade (Code) 'A'
       Grade (Code) 'A' has Translation (Category) 'Excellent'

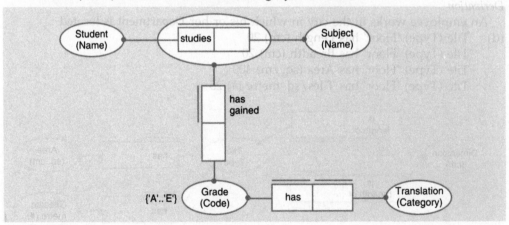

(b)    Student (#) 1023 has (Name) 'F. Gold'
       Student (#) 1023 has Gender (Code) 'F'
       Student (#) 1023 studies Subject (Name) 'English'

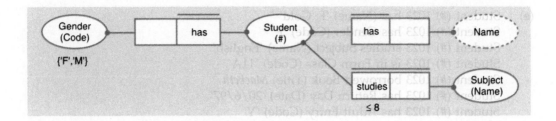

(c)  Student (#) 1023 has (Name) 'F. Gold'
Student (#) 1023 is in Form Class (Code) '11A'
Student (#) 1023 borrowed Book (Title) *Macbeth*
Student (#) 1023 has Return Day (Date) '20/6/97'

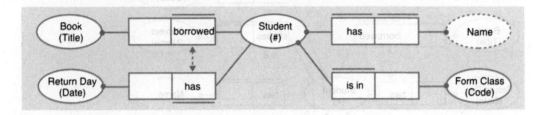

(d)  Student (#) 1023 has (Name) 'F. Gold'
Student (#) 1023 is in Form Class (Code) '11A'
Student (#) 1023 has Adult Entry (Code) 'Y'
Student (#) 1024 has Guardian (Name) 'Mr & Mrs N. Black'
Student (#) 1023 has Attendance (Type) 'F/T'
Student (#) 1023 has Car (Registration) 'OAS234'
Attendance (Type) 'F/T' has Translation (Category) 'Full time'

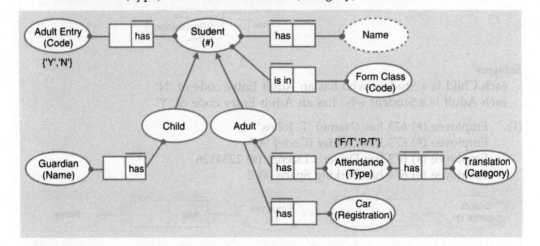

*Subtypes*
each Child is a Student who has an Adult Entry code of 'N'
each Adult is a Student who has an Adult Entry code of 'Y'

(e)    Student (#) 1023 has (Name) 'F. Gold'
       Student (#) 1023 has Gender (Code) 'F'
       Student (#) 1023 studies Subject (Name) 'English'
       Student (#) 1023 is in Form Class (Code) '11A'
       Student (#) 1023 borrowed Book (Title) *Macbeth*
       Student (#) 1023 has Return Day (Date) '20/6/97'
       Student (#) 1023 has Adult Entry (Code) 'Y'
       Student (#) 1024 has Guardian (Name) 'Mr & Mrs N. Black'
       Student (#) 1023 has Attendance (Type) 'F/T'
       Student (#) 1023 has Car (Registration) 'OAS234'
       Attendance (Type) 'F/T' has Translation (Category) 'Full time'

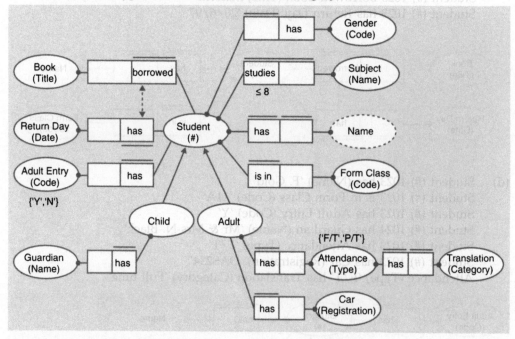

*Subtypes*
    each Child is a Student who has an Adult Entry code of 'N'
    each Adult is a Student who has an Adult Entry code of 'Y'

(f)    Employee (#) 673 has (Name) 'T. Johns'
       Employee (#) 673 has Gender (Code) 'M'
       Employee (#) 673 has Driver's Licence (#) 1234126
       Employee (#) 674 has Parking Space (#) 2

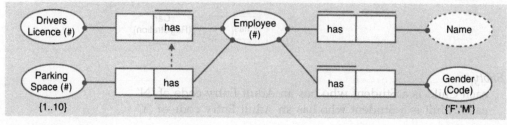

(g)  Event (Name) '100M' for Age (#) 13 has Athlete (Name) 'Q. Green'
     Event (Name) '100M' for Age (#) 13 has Time (sec) 12.3
     Event (Name) '100M' for Age (#) 13 has Distance (metre) 10.3

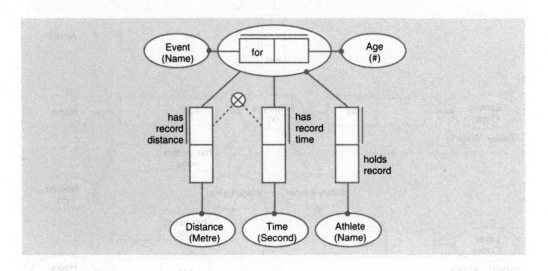

## EXERCISE 17

### Question 1

(a)  Employee (#) 001 has (Name) 'T. Mackay'
     Employee (#) 001 is paid Earning (Type) 'Salary'
     Employee (#) 002 has Hourly Rate ($) 13.67
     Employee (#) 002 has Hours (#) 40
     Employee (#) 001 has Level (Code) 'AD03'
     Employee (#) 001 receives Weekly Pay ($) 546.80
     Car (#) 1 has (Make) 'Mitsubishi'
     Car (#) 1 has (Model) 'Magna'
     Car (#) 1 has (Registration) '387 DAJ'
     Car (#) 1 driven by Employee (#) 001

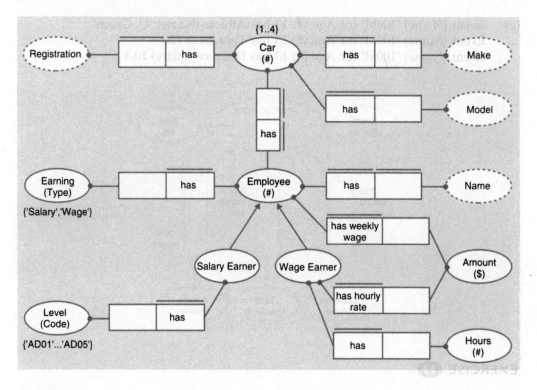

*Subtypes*

each Salary Earner is an Employee who has an Earning Type of 'Salary'
each Wage Earner is an Employee who has an Earning Type of 'Wage'

(b)  Element (Atomic #) 2 has (Name) 'Helium'
Element (Atomic #) 3 in Form (Type) 'metal' has Hardness (#) 0.6
Element (Atomic #) 2 in Form (Type) 'gas' has Molecule (Formula) 'He'
Element (Atomic #) 3 in Form (Type) 'metal' has Melting Point (°C) 179
Element (Atomic #) 2 in Form (Type) 'gas' has Boiling Point (°C) −269

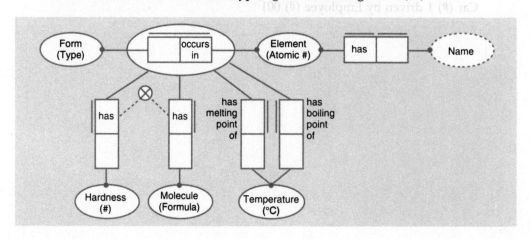

*Assumption*
Two forms of elements could have the same hardness, boiling or melting points

(c)    Customer (#) 001 has (Name) 'J. Green'
Customer (#) 001 on Day (Date) '30/6/97' had Treatment (Type) 'Cut'
Customer (#) 001 on Day (Date) '30/6/97' was done by Employee (Name) 'Jessie'

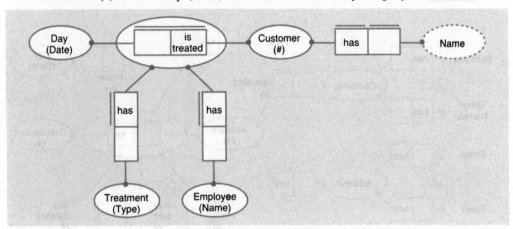

(d)    Car (Registration) '234 ASC' was built in Year (#) 1996
Car (Registration) '234 ASC' has (Description) 'Nissan Pulsar Sedan'
Car (Registration) '234 ASC' has Used (Code) 'Y'
Car (Registration) '234 ASC' has Odometer (Kilometre) 24 234
Car (Registration) '234 ASC' costs Price ($) 15 954

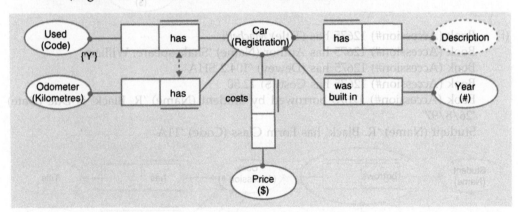

(e)    Account (#) 18276326 operated by Customer (Surname) 'Addams' and (Other Names) 'Marie Louise'
Account (#) 18276326 has Address (Street) '25 Gomez St' and (Town) 'Lurchville'
Account (#) 18276326 has Transaction (#) 2
Transaction (#) 2 for Account (#) 18276326 was on Day (Date) '30/6/97'
Transaction (#) 2 for Account (#) 18276326 was (Type) 'Deposit'
Transaction (#) 2 for Account (#) 18276326 has Credit ($) 123.95

Transaction (#) 3 for Account (#) 18276326 has Debt ($) 50.00
Transaction (#) 2 for Account (#) 18276326 has Current Balance ($) 208.80
**Note:** a transaction number was introduced here as no unique identifier could be found for a transaction, that is, it is possible in the same account, on the same day, to have two transactions of the same type and amount giving the same balance.

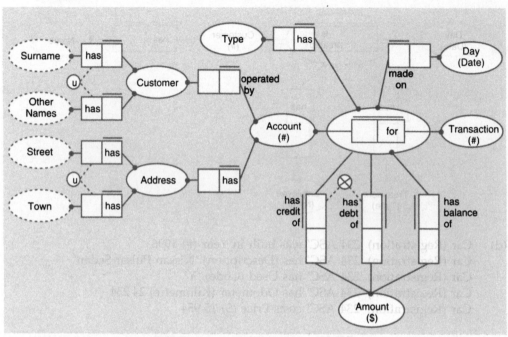

(f)    Book (Accession#) 12675 has (Title) *Macbeth*
Book (Accession#) 12675 has Author (Name) 'Shakespeare, William'
Book (Accession#) 12675 has (Dewey) '104.2 SHA'
Book (Accession#) 12675 has Cost ($) 12.50
Book (Accession#) 12675 borrowed by Student (Name) 'R. Black' is Due (Date) '26/8/97'
Student (Name) 'R. Black' has Form Class (Code) '11A'

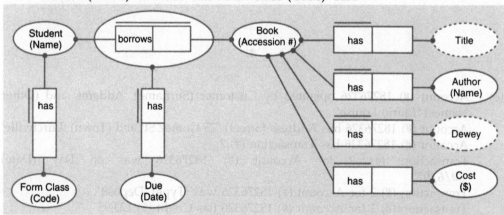

## EXERCISE 18

### Question 1

(a) Pizzas (<u>Name</u>, Size)
    Prices (<u>Size</u>, Cost)

(b) Locations (<u>Teacher, Subject, Room</u>)

(c) Prime Minister Details (<u>Name</u>, Birth Year, Death Year)

(d) Classes (<u>Subject, Student</u>, Teacher, Room)

(e) Fishing (<u>Location, Fish</u>)

Places (<u>Name,</u> Code, Longitude, Latitude)

(f)

Members (<u>Name</u>, Number, Expires, Manages)
    OP        OP

Teams (<u>Team, Day, Member</u>)

(g)

Enrolment (<u>Surname, Other names</u>, Country, DOB, Start Year, Religion, Street, Suburb,
        Entry Level, Home Phone, Guardian Phone)        OP
        OP            OP

Postcodes (<u>Suburb</u>, Postcode)

(h) Separation chosen as method.

                            {'Y','N'}
Student (<u>Number</u>, Name, Form Class, Adult)

Children (<u>Student#</u>, Guardian)

                {'F/T','P/T'}
Adults (<u>Student#</u>, Attendance, Car)
                            OP

Attendance (<u>Code</u>, Translation)

(i)     Separation chosen as method.

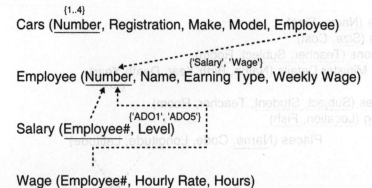

{1..4}

Cars (Number, Registration, Make, Model, Employee)

Employee (Number, Name, Earning Type, Weekly Wage)

{'Salary', 'Wage'}

{'ADO1', 'ADO5'}

Salary (Employee#, Level)

Wage (Employee#, Hourly Rate, Hours)

## Question 2

(a)     Album (Name) 'Black and White' is by Artist (Name) 'Michael Iron'
        Album (Name) 'Black and White' has Stock (#) 10
        Album (Name) 'Black and White' costs Price ($) 29.95
        Song (Name) 'Black and White' is sung by Artist (Name) 'Michael Iron' on Album
        (Name) 'Black and White'

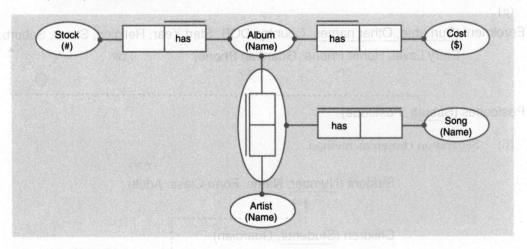

Albums (Name, Stock, Cost)

Songs (Album, Artist, Song)

(b)     Subject (Code) 'IT100' has (Name) 'Info Systems 1'
        Subject (Code) 'IT100' has Contact (Type) 'L' in Quantity (#) 2
        Subject (Code) 'IT100' has Credit (Points) 10
        Subject (Code) 'IT100' is offered in Year (#) 1997
        Subject (Code) 'IT100' occurs in Semester (#) 1
        Subject (Code) 'IT100' has Lecturer (Surname) 'Green'
        Year (#) 1997 in the Subject (Code) 'IT100' has Contact (Type) 'L' in Room (#) 23

Year (#) 1997 in the Subject (Code) 'IT100' has Contact (Type) 'L' at Time (Code) 'Mon. 10am'

Meeting (Type) 'L' has Translation (Type) 'Lecture'

Student (#) 47346 has (Surname) 'Green'

Student (#) 47346 has (First Name) 'Judy'

Student (#) 47346 is studying Course (Title) 'Dip IT'

Student (#) 47346 has Date of Birth (Day) '12.10.79'

Student (#) 47346 is enrolled in Subject (Code) 'IT100' in Year (#) 1996 and received Result (#) 6

Lecturer (Surname) 'Green' has (First Name) 'Robyn'

Lecturer (Surname) 'Green' has (Title) 'Dr'

Lecturer (Surname) 'Green' has Department (Name) 'Computer Science'

Lecturer (Surname) 'Green' has Phone (#) 2376

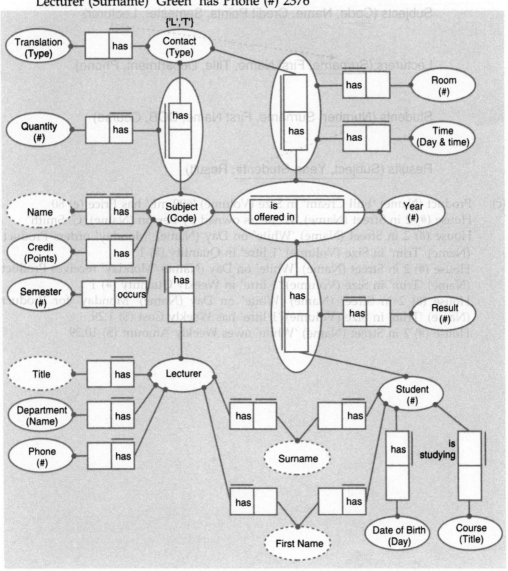

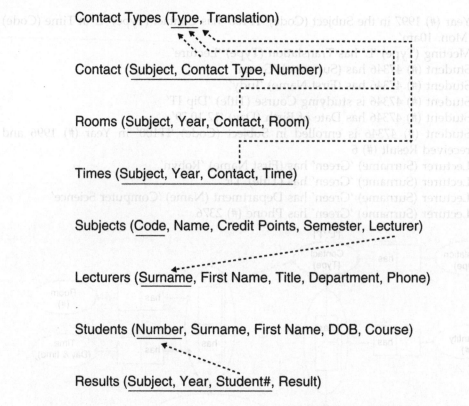

Contact Types (Type, Translation)

Contact (Subject, Contact Type, Number)

Rooms (Subject, Year, Contact, Room)

Times (Subject, Year, Contact, Time)

Subjects (Code, Name, Credit Points, Semester, Lecturer)

Lecturers (Surname, First Name, Title, Department, Phone)

Students (Number, Surname, First Name, DOB, Course)

Results (Subject, Year, Student#, Result)

(c)    Product (Name) 'Full Cream' in Size (Volume) '600 mL' has Price (¢) 80
House (#) 2 in Street (Name) 'White' is owned by Person (Name) 'G. Smith'
House (#) 2 in Street (Name) 'White' on Day (Name) 'Monday' orders Product
(Name) 'Trim' in Size (Volume) '1 litre' in Quantity (#) 1
House (#) 2 in Street (Name) 'White' on Day (Name) 'Monday' receives Product
(Name) 'Trim' in Size (Volume) '1 litre' in Weekly Quantity (#) 1
House (#) 2 in Street (Name) 'White' on Day (Name) 'Monday' for Product
(Name) 'Trim' in Size (Volume) '1 litre' has Weekly Cost ($) 1.29
House (#) 2 in Street (Name) 'White' owes Weekly Amount ($) 10.29

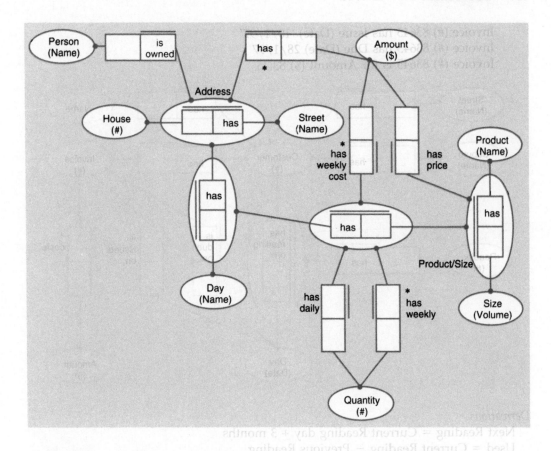

*Derivations*

Weekly Quantity = sum of Daily quantities for that Product/Size
Weekly Product Cost = weekly quantity × cost of that Product/Size
Weekly Cost for an Address = sum of Weekly Product Costs for that Address

*Relational schema*

Owners (<u>House, Street</u>, Person)
Orders (<u>House, Street, Day, Product, Size</u>, Quantity)
Prices (<u>Product, Size</u>, Cost)

*Derivations*

Weekly Quantity = sum of Daily quantities for that Product/Size
Weekly Product Cost = Weekly Quantity × cost of that Product/Size
Weekly Cost for an Address = sum of Weekly Product Costs for that Address

(d)    Customer (#) 3948743 has (Name) 'Ms G. Green'
       Customer (#) 3948743 has Street (Name) '4 White Street'
       Customer (#) 3948743 has Suburb (Name) 'Rainbowville'
       Customer (#) 3948743 on Reading (Date) '8/1/97' had Reading (#) 1725
       Customer (#) 3948743 on Reading (Date) '8/1/97' has Used (#) 120
       Customer (#) 3948743 on Reading (Date) '8/1/97' has MJs Used (#) 4723
       Customer (#) 3948743 received Invoice (#) 83645

Invoice (#) 83645 has Issue (Date) '10/1/97'
Invoice (#) 83645 has Due (Date) 28/1/97
Invoice (#) 83645 is for Amount ($) 83.35

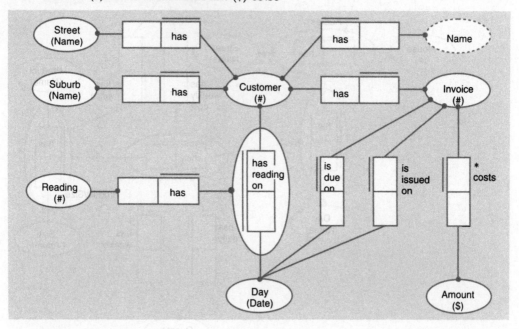

*Derivations*

Next Reading = Current Reading day + 3 months

Used = Current Reading − Previous Reading

MJs Used = Used × 39.36

Amount = if MJs Used < 1824 then MJs Used × 2.308 ÷ 100

if MJs Used > 1824 and MJs Used < 3648 then 42.10 + (MJs Used − 1824) × 1.532 ÷ 100

if MJs Used > 3648 then 70.04 + (MJs Used − 3648) × 1.242 ÷ 100

Customer (Number, Name, Street, Suburb)

Readings (Customer#, Day, Reading)

Invoices (Invoice#, Issued, Due, Customer)

# Index

arity 11
    binary 11
    quaternary 12
    ternary 24
    unary 11
arity check 37, 50
assumptions 17, 52
binary relationship 11, 16
combining entity types 32–5
conceptual information processor 2, 4
conceptual schema 1
conceptual schema design procedure 10
conceptual schema diagram (CSD) vi
constraints 2, 3
    disjunctive mandatory role 63–5, 92
    equality 80, 92
    exclusion 81–2, 92
    frequency 79, 92
    mandatory 60–1, 91
    subset 79–80, 92
    subtype 82–3
    uniqueness 37–42, 45, 46, 48, 58, 91, 93, 94
    value 78, 92
database vi
derivation rules 2, 3
derived facts 72–6
    arithmetic 72–3
    logical 74–6
elementary facts 10, 11, 12, 14, 21
entity 13
entity type 13, 21
    combining 32–5
equality constraints 80–1
exclusion constraints 81–2
external consistency 86
external schema 2
fact type(s) 21–6
    multiple 24–6
    nested 95–6
    one-to-one 96–7
    ternary 23–4
foreign key 91, 92
frequency constraints 79, 92
Halpin, Dr T.A. vi
internal schema 2
internal consistency 86
key 91

foreign 91, 92
    primary 91
logical schema 1
mandatory constraints 60
multiple fact types 24–5
Natural language Information Analysis Method
    (NIAM) vi
nested entity type 23–4
nested fact type 95
nesting 23–4
null value 60
Nijssen, Professor G.M. vi
Object-Role Modelling (ORM) vi, 10
one-to-one fact type 96–7
Optimal Normal Form (ONF) algorithm 93
population check 30–1
primary key 91
quaternary relationship 12
redundancy 37
reference scheme 1, 2, 13, 21
    compound 70–1
    primary 69–70
relational implementation 90
relational mapping procedure 93
relational schema 91
role 21
significant output report 16, 17
stored fact types 2, 3
subset constraints 79–80
subtype constraints 82–3
subtypes 97–8
supertype 82
ternary facts 23–4
ternary relationship 12, 17
transaction 4
unary relationship 11, 16
uniqueness constraints 37–42, 91, 93, 94
    external 58–9
    many-to-many situation 46–7
    one-to-many situation 45–6
    one-to-one situation 46
    assigned to nested fact types 48
universe of discourse (UoD) vi
universe of discourse expert vi
value constraints 78
values 3, 13